01928 508605

to

Children with Special Educational Needs

SECOND EDITION

Michael Alcott

WITHDRAWN

Hodder & Stoughton

A MEMBER OF THE HODDER HEADLINE GROUP

Orders: please contact Bookpoint Ltd, 130 Milton Park, Abingdon, Oxon OX14 4SB. Telephone: (44) 01235 827720. Fax: (44) 01235 400454. Lines are open from 9.00 – 6.00, Monday to Saturday, with a 24 hour message answering service. Email address: orders@bookpoint.co.uk

British Library Cataloguing in Publication Data
A catalogue record for this title is available from the British Library

ISBN 0 340 84818 9

First Published 1997
Second Edition published 2002
Impression number   10 9 8 7 6 5 4 3 2 1
Year   2007 2006 2005 2004 2003 2002

Cover photo from the John Birdsall Photo Library
Typeset by Fakenham Photosetting Limited, Fakenham, Norfolk
Printed in Great Britain for Hodder & Stoughton Educational, a division of Hodder Headline Plc, 338 Euston Road, London NW1 3BH by Martins the Printers, Berwick-upon-Tweed.

Contents

Acknowledgements

In writing this book I have drawn upon experience stretching back over many years. It is impossible to remember and acknowledge all the children, their parents and colleagues in schools who have contributed to my understanding of children who have special educational needs.

That said, I should like to express special thanks to the children, staff and parents of Green Hedges School, Cambridge. This school was opened in 1974. Built in response to the Education Act 1970, it was a symbol of a very important shift in society's attitude towards children with severe learning difficulties. Or, as they were then labelled, 'mentally handicapped' children.

If I ever felt low during my time there I only had to cast my mind back to the days before 1970. Then, all the children who were at Green Hedges School would have been deemed not worthy of education. I acknowledge and welcome the change.

★★★

Thanks to Elizabeth Tribe, Editorial Director at Hodder & Stoughton Educational.

The publishers would like to acknowledge the following picture agencies for granting permission to use copyright material in this book:

Topham Picturepoint p.1, p.4
Press Association p.3
Popperfoto p.6
Richard and Sally Greenhill p.8, p.10 (bottom), p.32 (top), p.40, p.79
David Townend p.10
John Birdsall Photo Library p.9, p.17, p.32 (bottom), p.49, p.58, p.60, p.62, p.64, p.72, p.74, p.76, p.78, p.84, p.87 (top), p.90, p.93, p.96, p.99 (top), p.108, p.113, p.130
Science Photo Library p.63, p.99 (bottom)
Format/Jacky Chapman p.128
Prior's Court School p.25, p.81 (top and bottom), p.85, p.87 (bottom), p.126

The statement of Special Educational Needs on pp.20–23 is from the Education (Special Education Needs) Regulations 1994. It is Crown copyright and is reproduced with permission from HMSO.

Introduction to Second Edition

It is five years since the first edition of *An Introduction to Children with Special Educational Needs* was published. In that time there have been a number of important developments and changes in the world of special educational needs (SEN). That first edition is out of date in significant ways.

This second edition is still only an introduction. It is intended for readers who may have little or no knowledge of children with SEN. I hope that it will provide you with some basic knowledge about the whole world of children with SEN. With that in place you can explore areas of your own interest.

The structure of this second edition is the same as the first edition. Chapter headings have been modified where appropriate. Some material has been added. Some has been deleted where it is no longer applicable. A number of small changes have been made to the text.

Some of the significant developments that have been brought into this edition include:

Special Educational Needs & Disability Act (2001)

This Act came into effect in January 2002. It focuses very much on inclusion. Inclusion has replaced Integration as a driving force in the education of children with SEN.

Revised SEN Code of Practice (2001)

The original Code (1994) provided schools with clear guidance on identifying and assessing children with SEN. The revised Code came into effect in January 2002.

OFSTED Inspection

The inspection of all schools by Ofsted inspectors has done much to change expectations for children with SEN and the curriculum in special schools. Still controversial.

Models of Disability

Awareness of different ways of considering people who have SEN has increased in recent years. The model that we hold dictates how we interact with people. As such, it is important for us to reflect on our own beliefs and attitudes.

Meeting SEN

The chapter entitled 'Educational Provision' has been expanded. Many ways of meeting the SEN of children and young adults cut across early years, primary, secondary, further and higher education. New material introduces some of the approaches available.

Activities

Some new ideas have been introduced as appropriate.

Further Reading

Some recent titles have been included.

Internet

The Internet is an excellent resource for finding information and keeping up to date on special educational needs. A brief list of useful websites has been included.

Addresses

These have been updated.

I hope that this second edition of *An Introduction to Children with Special Educational Needs* will provide you with a helpful introduction to a most important aspect of education.

Michael Alcott

Introduction

The purpose of this book is to introduce you to the world of children who have special educational needs (SEN). It is a basic text, not an academic work.

As such, it might be of help to the following readers:

- students who are studying courses where basic knowledge about children with SEN is a requirement
- people considering a career in which they will work with children who have SEN
- staff, perhaps recently appointed, who would like to have a broader view of things and see where they fit in.

The idea for the book developed when I was working as Deputy Head Teacher of a special school. Students from local schools, further education (FE) colleges and universities used to come to our school on work experience. It was my responsibility to supervise them.

Over the years it became apparent that these students fell into two groups: the confident and the terrified. Age didn't really matter. A 15-year-old from a local comprehensive could breeze in, bubbling with confidence. A mature student, maybe a mother, could sit in my office quivering like a jelly.

Why the difference? It often came down to personal experience, knowledge and familiarity. If the young student had, say, a brother or sister with SEN then that was usually enough to give him confidence. On the other hand, the mature student who had no experience or knowledge of children with SEN was facing the unknown. And that could cause serious anxiety.

Well then, I thought, what about a simple book that will introduce readers to children who have SEN? A book that might dispel some of the anxiety and promote confidence. This book grew from that idea.

The main point that I would like to get over in this book is this: a child who has SEN is an individual. He is Robert; she is Carole. It is important to get it right when we talk about children who have SEN. The way we talk about children reveals our attitudes to them. And attitude decides how we interact, how we value and how we educate children.

There are three words that often cause some difficulty:

- impairment
- disability
- handicap.

It is not always easy to get these words right. It is worth trying to understand them and learn how to use them correctly. They appear often in this book. Just take a moment. Say to yourself, 'Robert has a disability' and then, 'Robert is handicapped.' They do convey different messages. So, let's take a look at these words.

Impairment refers to a loss or abnormality of development or growth: a boy whose brain has been damaged may be left with an impairment of brain function. The nature of the impairment will depend on which area of the brain is damaged.

Disability refers to the limitation of activity caused by the impairment. A boy who has a motor impairment (caused by damage to the brain) may then have a disability in walking.

Handicap is the personal disadvantage that a person experiences in a particular society. Handicap is not in the person; it is in the social setting. A person with a visual disability may have a handicap when it comes to crossing busy roads.

As I say, it is not always easy to get the words right all the time. It is important to work at it. You can look at it like this: you can do nothing about a person's impairment. You can take note of a person's disability. You can respond to the disability and ensure that the person does not experience a handicap.

Whilst talking of words I will clarify the approach to the 'he-she'/'his-her' dilemma. I did start out using both 'he' and 'she' all over the place. Quite honestly, things got into a tangle. For the sake of simplicity, therefore I have decided to use the masculine form where gender is not a significant factor.

What do we mean by 'special educational needs'?

Here is an abbreviated official definition:

Children have special education needs if they have a learning *difficulty* which calls for *special educational provision* to be made for them.

(Section 312, Education Act 1996)

A child has a *learning difficulty* if he is not learning at roughly the same pace as other children in the same age group and school. He may have a disability which hinders learning. These two aspects also apply to pre-schoolers.

Special educational provision is by comparison with the provision for other children.

Now, let me explain briefly the contents of the book. I stress that it is a basic, simple introduction to a complex field.

Chapter 1: Legislation and guidance

This may sound a rather dry start to a book. Perhaps so, but there is no way round it. Since 1970 the lives of children with SEN have been transformed. Legislation has forced the transformation. The legislation provides the framework within which to place the many changes that have taken place.

Chapter 2: Some children with special educational needs

Here we look at the range of SEN and meet some individual children.

Chapter 3: Conditions that may cause learning difficulties

This is a list and description of some of the many conditions that can lead to learning difficulties.

Chapter 4: Meeting Special Educational Needs

This covers provision, including early years settings, mainstream primary and secondary, special schools, further education and the independent sector.

Chapter 5: Some people who work with children who have special educational needs

Here we meet some of the great range of staff who are involved in the education of children with SEN. This includes teachers, learning support assistants, early years workers, nursery nurses, therapists, educational psychologists. There are job descriptions and some interviews.

Chapter 6: Issues to consider
There are some subjects that always seem to be controversial; other issues arise and win all-round support. In this book we will take a look at integration, equal opportunities, advocacy, exceptionally able children, post-19 provision, teacher training.

The book is rounded off with a reading list, web sites and a list of addresses.

Where appropriate, Questions and Activities have been provided at the end of each chapter. These may help to consolidate and deepen your knowledge.

1

Legislation and Guidance

Legislation provides the legal structures within which we live together in society. As attitudes change, so legislation changes. Since 1970 there have been very important changes in legislation on Education. In broad terms, we can say that *all* children are now given the opportunity to go to school, to receive an education that is appropriate for them and to enjoy the fullest possible participation in social life.

Things were not always so. Before 1970 some children were considered ineducable. They were labelled 'mentally handicapped' – a term which is no longer acceptable in educational circles. These children were the responsibility of the health authorities. They were often cared for in long-stay hospitals or homes. Some attended training centres – places where social training and light work took place. Then came The Education (Handicapped Children) Act 1970. And with it the transformation of the quality of life for thousands of young people.

Education (Handicapped Children) Act 1970

The Act pulled no punches. *All* children were to be educated. No child would be considered ineducable. There were thousands of children in

training centres, special care units, hospitals and private homes. They were all to become the responsibility of local education authorities (LEAs).

The Act paved the way for many special schools to be built in the 1970s to accommodate the influx of pupils. This was a marvellous development. Schools were opened. Staff were trained. The life experiences of thousands of 'hidden' children were enhanced through education.

Throughout the 1970s the movement to educate all children gathered momentum. The new special schools were thriving. But by the end of the decade the philosophy had moved on. Integration became the buzz word. Enthusiastic educationists and many parents campaigned to have all children educated with their peers. Segregation was wrong, 'Close the special schools' became the new slogan.

The driving force behind this campaign for integration was The Warnock Report. We will now take a look at this major study of children with special educational needs (SEN).

The Warnock Report 1978

This was a most important document. Its full title was:

SPECIAL EDUCATIONAL NEEDS
Report of the Committee
of Enquiry into the
Education of Handicapped
Children and Young People
Chairman: Mrs H. M. Warnock

A Committee, chaired by Mrs Mary Warnock (now Baroness), spent four years investigating the education of 'handicapped children and young people'. Their Report was presented to Parliament in 1978. This Report has had a major impact on the education of children with SEN. Many of its recommendations became law in the Education Act 1981.

The Committee carried out a thorough review of educational provision in England, Scotland and Wales for children and young people who were 'handicapped by disabilities of body or mind'. A glance at the contents of the Report shows how comprehensive the study was. It includes the following subjects:

- the historical background
- a proposal to drop categorisation (i.e., labelling people according to broad categories such as 'delicate', 'educationally sub-normal')
- the introduction of the concept of special educational need
- assessment
- provision for under-fives
- the range of special educational needs
- integration
- the role of special schools
- the involvement of parents
- the transition from school to adult life
- curricular considerations
- the needs of different children
- teacher education
- the role of the advisory service, health and social services

and much more.

Baroness Warnock

As you can see, it was a wide-ranging and in-depth review of provision packed with many ideas for change and development.

We will now look at some of the most important aspects of this Report. Please bear in mind that we are talking about a study that was done in the mid-1970s. Since then there have been more developments. We shall consider some of these further on.

Special educational need (SEN)

This key concept, so familiar to us now, was introduced by the Report. The aim was to get rid of the idea of 'handicap'. This general label gave no idea about a person's needs nor of how they might be met.

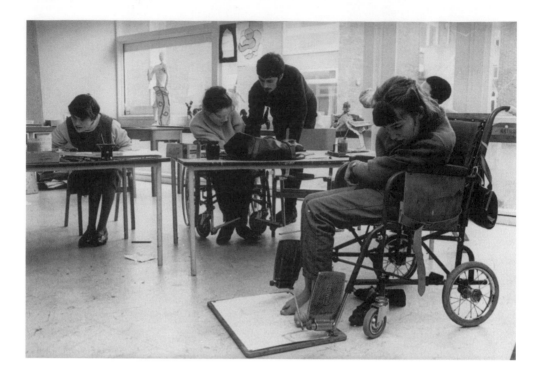

It was hoped that the change of concept would focus attention on a person's educational needs. These needs could be of three kinds:

- the need for special means of access to the curriculum
- modifications to the curriculum
- consideration of the environment in which a child was being educated, in particular the emotional and social aspects of that environment.

Special educational need was not something a person necessarily had for life. It was estimated that about 20% of all children could have SEN at some time during their school career. Long-term needs could arise from a major impairment. Short-term needs might arise from such things as:

- an accident or illness
- a long absence from school
- particular difficulty with one subject
- change of school
- temporary emotional problems.

The introduction of this new concept, now often referred to just as SEN, meant the end of categorisation and a focus on the individual. Before the Warnock Report, the child population was broadly divided into two groups:

the handicapped and the non-handicapped. It was common enough to hear somebody say, 'Oh, he's handicapped, you know.' Once handicapped, always handicapped. With it came a cluster of rather negative or condescending attitudes towards the child and a limited range of expectations.

Categorisation went further. Children were put into separate boxes. For example, they were labelled and known as The Blind, The Deaf, The Mentally Handicapped, and so on. The label focused all attention on a person's disability. Individuality was ignored. This was very useful for administrative purposes but not for the children who had to struggle to assert their individual identities.

Categorisation made educational provision a fairly straightforward matter. The Deaf were despatched to schools for The Deaf. The Blind were admitted to schools for The Blind. The Mentally Handicapped, who were considered ineducable, were sent off to hospitals or training centres.

If you want to see how things used to be, do take a look at the book *Out of Sight* by S. Humphries and P. Gordon (see Further Reading for details). There are photographs and snippets of life stories in there to make you weep.

The trouble with this tidy system was that it did not correspond to the reality of individual children's lives. In the 1960s I was teaching at a day school for The Physically Handicapped. Many of the children had some degree of paralysis as a consequence of a disease, poliomyelitis, also known as infantile paralysis. Looking back, I am amazed that so many of those children were segregated into a special school, because academically, they were as able as many children in mainstream schools. But in those days we all accepted categorisation and segregation.

Getting rid of such simple and unhelpful categorisation was one of the greatest achievements of the Warnock Report.

But what to put in its place? The Committee gave much time and thought to this. It was recognised that a child's disabilities could be multiple and complex. A child could have a hearing impairment along with a physical disability and, quite possibly, difficulties of an intellectual nature. A child might have a problem with reading, which could lead to emotional problems. A child might have a serious medical condition which could mean limited attendance at school which, in turn, could leave the child way behind his peers in learning.

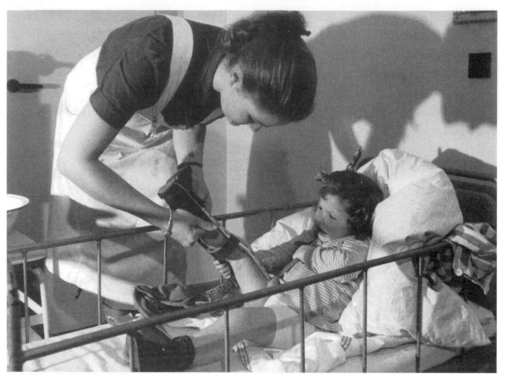

Putting on leg calipers

So, some new terms were introduced. It was hoped that they would give a more helpful description of a child's condition, acknowledge the complexity of such a condition and suggest an educational solution. The Report came up with the following ideas:

- visual disability and hearing disability
- speech and language disorders
- emotional and behavioural disorders
- learning difficulties – specific, mild, moderate and severe.

Since the late 1970s the terms have been modified and fine-tuned. We shall look at the current terms when we come to later legislation.

Discovery, assessment and recording

Since the Education Act 1944 there was legislation in place to ensure that children who had disabilities would be identified, diagnosed and provided with appropriate education. The Warnock Committee suggested some important changes to those procedures. Here are some of the key proposals:

- the earliest possible identification and diagnosis was essential. That is to say, from birth
- a medical examination, on its own, was not enough to identify a child's needs. There could be a case for psychological, educational and social examination; also, in some instances, examination by a specialist therapist. This multi-professional assessment would give a richer and far more detailed picture of an individual child's needs
- a five-stage model for assessment was proposed. We shall look at this in more detail when we consider the Code of Practice
- there should be an annual review of a child's SEN
- some changes in the recording procedures were proposed to ensure that a complete statement was made about the child's needs.

Children under five

The importance of educational provision for children with SEN at the earliest possible age was stressed. The parents were the main educators of very young children. They were to be given strong support. Parents were to be allocated a named Person to represent them, usually a health visitor. Home teachers should visit parents in their homes.

The Report emphasised the importance and value of such facilities as toy libraries, parents' workshops, playgrounds, opportunity groups and day nurseries.

The range of SEN and provision

The Report stressed that there was a continuum of special educational needs. Any one child could have a complex set of needs. If such complex needs were to be met then it followed that the educational provision would need to be varied and flexible. The range could include:

- full-time education in a mainstream class with some support
- education in a specialised unit on a mainstream site
- special schools
- home tuition.

There would be plenty of scope for variety and flexibility in this range of provision.

Integration

The integration of children with SEN into mainstream schools had been government policy long before the Warnock Report. However, the

Committee gave a lot of time and attention to the varied ways in which children might be educated in integrated settings. The emphasis was on educating all children together, as long as the needs of all pupils could be met in this way.

What exactly is 'integration'? The concept is slippery. Every since the Warnock Report highlighted the importance of integration there has been debate about the meaning of the word. What exact experiences are integrated? What do children get out of integration? The Report started by proposing that there were three main levels of integration:

- location
- social
- functional.

We will look at these more closely.

LOCATION

This is the most basic type of integration. Children with SEN are educated at the same location or site as their peers. They might be located in a classroom or separate unit on a secondary school site; they might be in a classroom or block of classrooms in a primary school.

It would be quite possible for the pupils with SEN to have no contact whatsoever with the rest of the pupils in the school. So what is the point? Not much, admittedly. Here are a few possible advantages:

- parents might like the arrangement
- pupils with SEN would be able to see and hear the other pupils even though they would not interact with them
- perhaps rather more significant, the mainstream pupils might develop an awareness of pupils with SEN. They would know that children with disabilities do actually exist and are part of their world.

SOCIAL

Social integration brings greater benefits for children. As well as being located on a mainstream site, children with SEN would meet other pupils in social situations. They might dine with them, join with them at playtimes, share in extra-curricular activities and so on.

It was felt that this arrangement might lead to the following gains:

- the mainstream children could be encouraged to understand and accept differences in people
- friendships might develop
- children with disabilities might grow up feeling accepted by other children and their families.

So often a child with SEN has few or no friends. Social integration could help to overcome this sad situation.

FUNCTIONAL

This is the fullest form of integration. As well as being educated on the same site and enjoying social activities together, children study together. They all participate in the curriculum and the full range of classroom activities. The children with SEN may spend some time apart for specialised teaching but a significant part of their education takes place with their mainstream peers.

Through the process of functional integration the following gains might occur:

- pupils with SEN might have the chance to maximise their achievements
- they could be fully accepted in the school community
- that acceptance could lead to full acceptance and participation in the wider community.

That was a high ambition. It is useful to understand these 3 levels of integration. They will help you to see the difference between integration and inclusion.

Special schools

Whilst the Report placed strong emphasis on integration, the Committee stated very clearly that there would always be a place in the education system for special schools. See Chapter 8 of the Report itself for details of this. Some children would need placement in a special school for a short time; others for the whole of their education. There would always be a need for both day and residential special schools.

It has to be said that some LEAs, fired up by their enthusiasm for integration, considered that there was no need for special schools. This was never the intention of the Report.

Parents

The Report recommended the fullest possible involvement of parents of children with SEN in all aspects of their assessment and education. The parents would need support in a variety of ways – in particular, information, advice and practical help. For some parents, that would mean involvement from the day their child was born.

Curricular considerations

The Report gave considerable space to the curriculum. The arrival of the National Curriculum in 1988 makes much of the Warnock Report's comments of limited value now. We can note that there was concern about special schools underestimating the abilities of pupils with SEN. There was also an emphasis on the key role played by school staff in ensuring high quality education.

Teacher education and training

All teachers may have to teach children who have SEN. One in five, remember, is the number of pupils who, according to the Report, will have

SEN at some time in their educational career. It follows that all teachers are teachers of pupils with SEN. This fact has important implications for teacher education and in-service training.

There should be a 'special education element' in all courses of initial training. This element should be delivered in the context of child development.

The Report goes into some detail in Chapter 12 about the aims of this element and the skills that teachers need to acquire. There is also comment on the way in which teachers might be able to gain specialist knowledge and skills so that they can concentrate on working with children who have specific needs. Basically, the Report sees special training as a bolt-on qualification after graduation as a teacher. In Chapter 6 on 'Issues' we shall look at this in greater detail.

The Warnock Report did not deal with training of child care students, many of whom go on to work alongside teachers. Training in SEN is now an integral part of all child care courses.

Other areas

There is much more of interest and importance in the Warnock Report. As mentioned earlier there are sections on transition from school to adult life, the advisory service, the role of health and social services. There are also sections on other staff, voluntary organisations, research, development and resources.

Hundreds of people gave evidence to the Committee. Their conclusions and recommendations are presented in the Report. The Warnock Report 1978 is a major document in the history of the education of children with SEN. Should you wish to look at the Report it should be available in any well-stocked public library – and certainly in the library of an FE or HE institution.

Education Act 1981

This Act was based on the findings of the Warnock Report. It is all about children with SEN. The responsibilities of LEAs are specified. Children who may have SEN are to be identified and assessed. The age of the child does not matter.

Under-twos, with the consent of parents, are eligible for assessment. If necessary, the LEA must provide the child with a statement of SEN. A statement is a legally binding document.

In the early days of statementing (as the process became known) LEAs plunged into the business with enthusiasm. Sometimes they discovered that they had committed themselves to making provision for a child that, in reality, they could not deliver. They lacked the resources and funding to meet requirements. This caused much frustration for parents. As a result, statements are now sometimes written in rather less precise terms.

The Act makes it clear that LEAs have a responsibility to make provision to meet a child's SEN. Special schools are defined as those schools where special provision is made to meet SEN. It all seems to go round in a circle.

One point to note is that special schools are an accepted part of the full range of provision for children with SEN. This is important for there has been much debate over the years about the need for such schools.

Education Reform Act 1988

This Act introduced the National Curriculum. Before 1988 schools could create their own curriculum. For special schools this was important. A special school could tailor the curriculum to meet the identified needs of the particular pupils in the school. The curriculum was driven by pupil needs. The National Curriculum, by contrast, by a subject-led approach. Teachers and some parents of pupils with SEN were very concerned about this.

The father of a boy with cerebral palsy said to me, 'Tony needs to spend time learning to feed, to toilet, to dress. There's no point in him doing things like science and technology before he can look after himself.' Many people expressed similar views. It seemed as if the pupils were to be fitted into a curriculum even if it did not address their needs.

No doubt sensing that there might be trouble of this nature, the Act makes two concessions. Children who have SEN may be excluded from the National Curriculum. If that is too extreme then they can have a modified provision. Temporary exclusion was an option for a child who had short-term needs, perhaps due to illness or long absence.

Much has happened since this Act. After the dust had settled, very few children with SEN were excluded from the National Curriculum. Teachers did not like the idea of opening a deep curricular chasm between children with SEN and their peers.

However, there are many staff working with children who have SEN who are still not convinced that the National Curriculum is appropriate for some children. Many still favour a needs-led curriculum. This debate will rumble on.

The Children Act 1989

This was a major piece of legislation. It brought in some very important legal changes concerning children. Here are some of the main points:

- The welfare of the child must be the first concern in any dispute or legal proceedings involving the child. The child must be kept informed of what is going on. His wishes must be considered at all times.
- Parents have responsibilities towards their children. The main responsibility is to bring up their children, ideally in a family setting. Parental responsibility lasts until a child is 18 years old.
- Local authorities must ensure the welfare of children in need. These needs refer to a child's health, education and general development. The authority must make sure that services are provided to meet the child's needs.
- The idea of 'looked-after children' is introduced. Children who are provided with accommodation by a local authority are 'looked-after children'.
- Care and supervision orders will be granted in response to a court application from social services or the NSPCC. Such an order gives parental responsibility to the local authority.
- The protection of children who have been or are likely to be abused is a major concern. Schools have a legal obligation to work with other agencies, especially social services, to ensure that any child protection investigation is carried out quickly and thoroughly.
- Child assessment orders and emergency protection orders may be granted to social services or the NSPCC.

Many other provisions are made by this important Act.

Further Education and Higher Education Act 1992

This Act focused on access to further and higher education for people in the 16–18 year age range. Access for people with SEN was extended to 25 years of age.

It's all very well to say that people with SEN should be encouraged and welcomed into colleges and universities. Special resources may be needed. This problem was to be addressed through The Further Education Funding Council (FEFC). Money was to be made available to provide resources as necessary. An important matter.

Education Act 1993

Amongst other things this Act had a focus on children with SEN. It promoted their inclusion in mainstream school. It emphasised the role of parents. They were to be fully involved in the choice of school for their child. If the parents disagreed with the LEA then they could appeal to a Special Educational Needs Tribunal. Such tribunals were developed from 1994.

The Act also led to the *Code of Practice on the Identification and Assessment of Special Educational Needs* in 1994.

Code of Practice 1994

NB The Code of Practice was revised in 2001. The Revised Code came into effect in January 2002. It is still useful to know details of the original Code. We shall consider the Revised Code in its chronological place.

The Code links with the SEN and Disability Act 2001 which also came into effect in January 2001. The following are some of the major developments in the new Code:

- emphasis on the inclusion of children with SEN in mainstream schools
- better links with parents
- better links between Education, Health and Social Services
- sections devoted to early years, primary and secondary phase of education
- involvement of children in assessment and decision-making.

If a child is considered in need of assessment for a Statement of SEN then five areas are to be taken into account:

- communication and interaction
- cognition and learning
- behaviour, emotional and social development
- sensory and/or physical needs
- medical conditions.

The revised Code does differ from the original in some important ways. It should work better for schools and lead to more efficient identification and assessment of children's SEN.

The full title of this important document is: Code of Practice on the Identification and Assessment of Special Educational Needs 1994. It is a substantial volume of some 150 A4 pages. It was prepared by the Department for Education.

The Code provides guidelines for LEAs on ways of making the best use of resources devoted to the education of children with SEN. It builds on the recommendations of the Warnock Report 1978, the Education Act 1981 and the Education Act 1993 in particular. The Code has been approved by Parliament.

Primary and secondary schools follow the guidelines. The Code is also recommended for use by the health services, social services and any other services concerned with the education of children with SEN.

Here we can look at some of the keys points of the Code. In the Introduction, some basic principles are set out. The main ideas are that:

- there is a continuum of needs and therefore of provision
- the curriculum must be broad and balanced
- mainstream provision is seen as the priority where possible
- identification of SEN before a pupil attends school is encouraged
- parents must be seen as partners with LEAs and other agencies.

As for actual practices and procedures, the Code highlights the following:

- early identification
- mainstream provision if possible

- LEAs to make multidisciplinary assessment and statement as needed
- annual review of a child's statement
- the child's views to be considered.

SEN policy

All schools must have a SEN policy. This policy must contain information on the following:

- the special educational provision made by the school
- how the school identifies, assesses and provides for children who have SEN
- the schools' policy on staffing, working with outside agencies and parents.

The special educational needs co-ordinator (SENCo)

All mainstream schools must have a SEN co-ordinator or a group of staff who form a SEN support team. The co-ordinator has a number of functions to perform. Among them are:

- ensuring that the school's SEN policy is implemented
- working with and advising colleagues
- co-ordinating provision
- dealing with administrative matters
- liaising with parents and external agencies
- making a contribution to the in-service training of staff.

All those functions have to be performed, along with a teaching responsibility. The Code urges school governors to ensure that the co-ordinator has appropriate time to perform this important role effectively.

Whilst stressing the importance of early identification, the Code emphasises close liaison with the parents. Wherever possible the child should also be involved in the process and should be allowed to give his views about possible provision. Should the school feel that further investigation of a child's needs is necessary, then the LEA must be brought on to the scene.

The five-stage model

This is a progressive model for identifying and assessing children who have SEN. Stages 1–3 take place in school; stages 4 and 5 involve the LEA.

STAGES 1 TO 3: SCHOOL-BASED STAGES OF ASSESSMENT AND PROVISION

It is emphasised that 20% of pupils have SEN at some time or other during their school career. It is the responsibility of the school governing body to ensure that pupils' SEN are met. Most pupils do have their needs met in mainstream school. Only about 2% of pupils require a statement of SEN. Such a statement is a legally binding document and the LEA must fulfil its recommendations.

STAGES 4 AND 5

About 2% of pupils may need a formal assessment of their SEN. This is a detailed, lengthy process that involves officers of the LEA. The Code sets out how LEAs should proceed, and includes time limits and criteria for making this formal assessment. This assessment, known as a statutory assessment, will become a legally binding statement.

Statutory assessment is a multidisciplinary activity. It can involve a wide range of input – parental, educational, medical, psychological, social. Reports can also come from any other agency nominated by the parents.

Schools are advised to use a list of criteria in deciding whether a formal, statutory assessment of a child's needs is necessary. If a child is not making appropriate academic progress than further enquiry is required. It will be important to establish what is causing a child's learning difficulty. The child's learning difficulty may be the outcome of one or more of the following:

- learning difficulties (moderate, severe or profound and multiple)
- specific learning difficulties (e.g. dyslexia)
- emotional and behavioural difficulties
- physical disabilities

- sensory impairment: hearing difficulties
- sensory impairment: visual difficulties
- speech and language difficulties
- medical conditions.

After making a full assessment the LEA must then decide if a formal statement of SEN is required. If the LEA considers that the pupil's mainstream school can meet his needs without additional resources, then no statement is needed. If it is felt that the school will need further resources or that a special school placement is preferable then a statement will be required.

Producing a statement is a lengthy business involving many hours of input from a wide range of professionals. There are six parts to a statement:

- introduction
- special educational needs
- special educational provision
- placement
- non-educational needs
- non-educational provision.

It is important for LEAs to get the statement right. It is a legal document and commits the LEA to make the appropriate provision for the pupil.

Whilst the SEN of many children will become apparent at school, some children will be identified as having SEN before they start school. The Code supports assessment for very young children. Early identification is important. Parents are to be fully involved in any decision making.

Annual review

Every year a child's statement must be reviewed. The review is carried out by school staff, other professionals involved with the child, and parents. Often, children are invited to attend their reviews.

The purpose of the review is to examine the previous year of education, to decide if any changes need to be made to the statement and to establish educational goals for the next year.

A particularly important annual review is the one immediately after a child's 14th birthday. A Transition Plan will be drawn up to ensure a satisfactory move from childhood to adulthood.

Pages 20–23 show a suggestion for the format of a statement offered by the Code.

PART B
STATEMENT OF SPECIAL EDUCATIONAL NEEDS

Part 1: Introduction

1. In accordance with section 168 of the Education Act 1993 ('the Act') and the Education (Special Educational Needs) Regulations 1994 ('the Regulations'), the following statement is made by [*here set out name of authority*] ('the authority') in respect of the child whose name and other particulars are mentioned below.

Child

Surname ....   Other names ....

Home address ....

....   Sex ....

....   Religion ....

Date of Birth ....   Home language ....

Child's parent or person responsible

Surname ....   Other names ....

Home address ....

....   Relationship to child ....

....

Telephone No. ....

2. When assessing the child's special educational needs the authority took into consideration, in accordance with regulation 10 of the Regulations, the representations, evidence and advice set out in the Appendices to this statement.

SPECIAL EDUCATIONAL NEEDS – REGULATIONS 27

PART 2: SPECIAL EDUCATIONAL NEEDS

[Here set out the child's special educational needs, in terms of the child's learning difficulties which call for special educational provision, assessed by the authority.]

PART 3: SPECIAL EDUCATIONAL PROVISION

Objectives

[Here specify the objectives which the special educational provision for the child should aim to meet.]

Educational provision to meet needs and objectives

[Here specify the special educational provision which the authority consider appropriate to meet the needs specified in Part 2 and to meet the objectives specified in this Part, and in particular specify –

(a) any appropriate facilities and equipment, staffing arrangements and curriculum,

(b) any appropriate modifications to the application of the National Curriculum,

(c) any appropriate exclusions from the application of the National Curriculum, in detail, and the provision which it is proposed to substitute for any such exclusions in order to maintain a balanced and broadly based curriculum; and

(d) where residential accommodation is appropriate, that fact].

Monitoring

[Here specify the arrangements to be made for –

(a) regularly monitoring progress in meeting the objectives specified in this Part,

(b) establishing targets in furtherance of those objectives,

(c) regularly monitoring the targets referred to in (b),

(d) regularly monitoring the appropriateness of any modifications to the application of the National Curriculum, and

(e) regularly monitoring the appropriateness of any provision substituted for exclusions from the application of the National Curriculum.

Here also specify any special arrangements for reviewing this statement.]

PART 4: PLACEMENT

[Here specify –

(a) *type of school which the authority consider appropriate for the child and the name of the school for which the parent has expressed a preference or, where the authority are required to specify the name of a school, the name of the school which they consider would be appropriate for the child and should be specified, or*

(b) *the provision for his education otherwise than at a school which the authority consider appropriate.]*

PART 5: NON-EDUCATIONAL NEEDS

[Here specify the non-educational needs of the child for which the authority consider provision is appropriate if the child is to properly benefit from the special educational provision specified in Part 3.]

PART 6: NON-EDUCATIONAL PROVISION

[Here specify any non-educational provision which the authority propose to make available or which they are satisfied will be made available by a district health authority, a social services authority or some other body, including the arrangements for its provision. Also specify the objectives of the provision, and the arrangements for monitoring progress in meeting those objectives.]

_____   _____

Date   A duly authorised officer of the authority

Appendix A: Parental Representations

[Here set out any written representations made by the parent of the child under section 167(1)(d) of or paragraph 4(1) of Schedule 10 to the Act and a summary which the parent has accepted as accurate of any oral representations so made or record that no such representations were made.]

Appendix B: Parental Evidence

[Here set out any written evidence either submitted by the parent of the child under section 167(1)(d) of the Act or record that no such evidence was submitted.]

Appendix C: Advice from the Child's Parent

[Here set out the advice obtained under regulation 6(1)(a).]

Appendix D: Educational Advice

[Here set out the advice obtained under regulation 6(1)(b).]

Appendix E: Medical Advice

[Here set out the advice obtained under regulation 6(1)(c).]

Appendix F: Psychological Advice

[Here set out the advice obtained under regulation 6(1)(d).]

Appendix G: Advice from the Social Services Authority

[Here set out the advice obtained under regulation 6(1)(e).]

Appendix H: Other Advice Obtained by the Authority

[Here set out the advice obtained under regulation 6(1)(f).]

6th April 1994	Eric Forth
Date	Parliamentary Under Secretary of State, Department for Education
7th April 1994	John Redwood
Date	Secretary of State for Wales

Disability Discrimination Act 1995

This Act has important messages for schools, further education (FE) colleges and institutions of higher education (HE). In the Act, disability is defined as 'a physical or mental impairment which has a substantial and long-term adverse effect on a person's ability to carry out normal day-to-day activities'.

Schools

With regard to school placement the Act states that LEAs have a duty to place children with SEN in a mainstream school, with the following provisos:

- the parents want the placement
- the placement is appropriate to the child's needs
- the education of other children is not affected
- resources are being used efficiently.

In addition schools must publish a SEN policy which is available for parents to read.

Thinking about the above statements, it is clear that there is plenty of scope for debate as to whether a particular child should or should not attend a mainstream school.

Further and higher education institutions

The Act states that these institutions must publish a Disability statement. The statement is to include information on the following with regard to students with disabilities:

- details of facilities
- access
- specialist equipment
- counselling provision.

The key point is the government's intention that children and adults with disabilities should have equal opportunities for education at all levels.

Education Act 1996

This Act brings together legislation from the Education Act 1944 up to the Education Act 1993. Part IV of Chapter 56 of the Act is 'Special Educational Needs'. Here you can find detailed information on legislation about the education of pupils who have SEN. The section is about 500 pages long. Here we will pick out some of the key points.

With regard to children who have SEN the Act covers the following:

- definition of SEN
- the Code of Practice
- special educational provision – general
- the identification and assessment of children with SEN
- Special Educational Needs Tribunal
- special schools.

Special educational needs in the Act

The Act state that a child has SEN if he has a learning difficulty which requires special provision to be made for him.

Learning difficulty

What is a learning difficulty? For the purpose of the Act there are two important ideas:

- A child may have difficulty in learning which is significantly greater than most children of his age.
- A child may have a disability which impedes learning.

It is stressed that if a child's home language is different from the one in which his education is delivered, this does not constitute a learning difficulty. You might like to think about that.

'Learning difficulty' is not an absolute condition. It is a relative concept. A child's difficulty is relative to the ability of others of his age and in his school. The relative nature of this concept means that there is plenty of scope for discussion and disagreement about individual cases.

Special educational provision

So, a child has SEN if he has a learning difficulty that requires special educational provision. What is this special educational provision? Again, it is a relative concept. If a child needs some kind of provision which is extra or different from that made for other children of his age in a LEA mainstream school then that is considered to be special educational provision.

Special needs tribunal

It may happen that parents will not agree with the LEA's assessment of their child. If so, they can go to the tribunal. It is an independent body which will examine the case and make a judgement.

Special schools

According to the Act a special school is one which makes special provision for children who have SEN. You might like to think about this distinction between special and mainstream schools. Later in the book we will be looking at the provision that is made by mainstream and special schools to meet the SEN of pupils.

National Curriculum

In the section on the National Curriculum there is a reference to those pupils who have statements of SEN. The Act states that such pupils may be excluded from the legal requirement to follow the National Curriculum, or that modifications may be made to the curriculum.

In reality, very few pupils are excluded from participation in the National

Curriculum. Pupils in special schools may follow a modified curriculum. There is a widespread feeling that if pupils are excluded they will be marginalised to such an extent that they will never be able to share in the curriculum with their peers.

Inclusive Learning: The Report of the Learning Difficulties and/or Disabilities Committee 1996

The report is often referred to as the Tomlinson Report after the name of the chairman. It is a significant report that promoted the inclusion of people with learning difficulties and/or disabilities in further education.

Excellence for All Children 1997

This Green Paper is subtitled 'Meeting Special Educational Needs'.

Inclusion is the key word in this document. What is meant by inclusion? Here is a statement from the Green Paper:
> 'Inclusion is a process not a fixed state. By inclusion, we mean not only that pupils with SEN should wherever possible receive their education in a mainstream school, but also that they should join fully with their peers in the curriculum and life of the school. (p.44)

The Paper acknowledges that a special school may be the best choice for a minority of pupils with SEN. Also, the wishes of parents are to be taken into account regarding choice of school.

This Paper opened up widespread debate on inclusion. Just as The Warnock Report sowed the seeds that led to the Education Act 1981, so this Green Paper sowed the seeds for the Special Educational Needs and Disability Act 2001.

Special Educational Needs and Disability Act 2001

This important Act focuses on Inclusion. It gives children with SEN the right to go to mainstream school. That said, there are two conditions:

- their parents want such a placement
- the education of other children is not affected adversely.

Schools are expected to make the necessary provision for children with SEN to access the curriculum. Where there appears to be discrimination against a child with SEN parents can take their case to the SEN Tribunal.

This body is to be renamed the Special Educational Needs and Disability Tribunal.

What happens to the child who fails the mainstream entry requirements? Probably, placement in a special school is the answer. So there will still be special schools in the whole range of educational provision. This is an important point. Some people feared that special schools would be swept away by the inclusion broom. Not so.

This Act promotes parent partnership schemes. Parents have sometimes felt left out of decision making about the education of their son or daughter. This Act insists that the role of parents must be strengthened.

The Special Educational Needs Code of Practice 2001

This revised version of the 1994 Code of Practice came into effect in January 2002.

The new Code gives guidance to schools on identifying, assessing and making provision for children's special educational needs. It includes early years, primary and secondary phases of education.

The Code links with the SEN and Disability Act 2001 which also came into effect in January 2001. The following are some of the major developments in the new Code:

- emphasis on the inclusion of children with SEN in mainstream schools
- better links with parents
- better links between Education, Health and Social Services
- sections devoted to early years, primary and secondary phases of education
- involvement of children in assessment and decision-making.

If a child is considered in need of assessment for a Statement of SEN then five areas are to be taken into account:

- communication and interaction
- cognition and learning
- behaviour, emotional and social development
- sensory and/or physical needs
- medical conditions.

The revised Code does differ from the original in some important ways. It should work better for schools and lead to more efficient identification and assessment of children's SEN.

We have now completed our overview of major legislation about children who have SEN. As you can see, since 1970 a lot of time and attention has been devoted to legislation about the 20% of pupils in our schools who have SEN. No doubt we shall continue to see changes and developments in furture years.

ACTIVITIES and QUESTIONS

1 Before the Education Act 1970 some children were considered 'ineducable'. Find out what happened to them. Discuss your findings with other students.
2 Familiarise yourself with the Warnock Report 1978.
3 Explain, in your own words, the concept of 'special educational need' (see Warnock).
4 What percentage of all pupils have SEN at some time during their school career?
5 What are your views on putting children into categories?
6 How does inclusion differ from integration?
7 If you are training to be a teacher find out about the Special Needs preparation in your college. Compare it with that offered in any other colleges. If you are a child care student you can find out about Special Needs preparation from the course syllabus. Discuss your findings with other students and tutors.
8 Why is The Children Act 1989 so important?
9 Familiarise yourself with 'The Code of Practice ... 1994'.
10 If you are on a placement or working in a school or nursery, read up the Special Educational Needs Policy.
11 What are some key points of the revised SEN Code of Practice (2001)?
12 If you are in a school or nursery, find out how many children have SEN. How many of them have a statement of SEN? As the SEN co-ordinator if you can see a statement.
13 Read up your FE or HE college's disability statement. Then discuss the quality of the provision.

2

Some Children with Special Educational Needs

The range of special educational needs

Academic attainment is the starting point for looking at SEN. If a child is not progressing and learning roughly at the same pace as his peers then there are grounds for concern. He has a learning difficulty. It may be temporary or permanent. It may be short-term or long-term.

The next step is to establish the cause or causes for the learning difficulty. That done, the nature of the child's SEN can be considered.

A pupil's level of attainment may be affected by many factors. These will include such things as attendance, medical condition, sensory impairment, psychological difficulties, home and social difficulties.

One of the problems of listing SEN is that there are some children whose needs are complex. For example, a child who has autism may have severe learning difficulties. On the other hand he may be quite bright. His behaviour may hinder his learning. So where do you put him? Bearing in mind the complexity of some children's needs we can adopt the list of SEN used in the 'Code of Practice':

LEARNING DIFFICULTIES
Moderate
Severe
Profound and Multiple

SPECIFIC LEARNING DIFFICULTIES
Dyslexia

EMOTIONAL AND BEHAVIOURAL DIFFICULTIES

PHYSICAL DISABILITIES

Sensory impairment: hearing difficulties

Sensory impairment: visual difficulties

Speech and language difficulties

Medical conditions

To this list we shall add one more:

Very able

It may seem strange to say that very able children, previously called 'gifted' have SEN. Able children do not usually have a learning difficulty. However, compared to their peers in a mainstream school these children do have special needs. They may need special provision. We shall consider exceptionally able children in Chapter 6 – Some Issues.

We can now look at each of these broad groups in turn.

Learning difficulties

As we have seen, learning difficulties can be described as *moderate*, *severe* or *profound and multiple*. These terms are usually abbreviated to MLD, SLD, PMLD respectively. Boundaries between these three degrees of learning difficulty are not clear-cut. The idea of *mild* learning difficulties is not often used although the Warnock Report introduced the idea.

All children with learning difficulties show academic attainment that is significantly below that of their peers in most subjects of the curriculum. They usually have serious problems with the basic skills of reading, writing and working with numbers.

Several factors may combine to cause the learning difficulty. There is often medical origin for the difficulty – especially for pupils who have either SLD or PMLD. Such pupils may have Down's syndrome, autism, cerebral palsy or one of many other conditions that can affect the level of intellectual ability. In addition, a child may have a sensory impairment, emotional and behavioural problems or problems of a more social nature, for example, in relating to people.

Depending on the severity and complexity of the child's disabilities, he will be described as having MLD, SLD or PMLD.

We can now meet some pupils with learning difficulties.

Peter – A boy with MLD

Peter is seven years old. He is a well-developed boy, strong and energetic. He is very physical: he loves charging about, kicking balls, climbing trees. He has two older brothers and he has plenty of rough and tumble with them. His father has been unemployed for many years. His mother has a part-time job as a cleaner.

The family live on an old local authority estate in an industrial area. It is rather run-down. Empty houses are boarded up. There is evidence of vandalism here and there. Unemployment of young men is high. There are no proper play areas other than a patch or two of worn grass.

Peter plays out with friends. They are a loosely knit gang and Peter admits that they enjoy roaming the streets. They climb into gardens, mess about with any discarded items of furniture such as sofas, washing machines, prams. Peter never has any real trouble with other boys. The local bullies steer clear of him. He knows who they are.

At home Peter shares a bedroom with one of his brothers, Ian. They get on OK. He can dress without help, usually choosing his own clothes for the day. In the morning he admits that he only has a quick wash. He does not bath very often. He has no difficulty eating or drinking. He does not like vegetables very much and rarely eats fruit. At school he has a free dinner.

At the local primary school he is in a mixed class of 30 pupils. He attends school regularly, in spite of the example of one his brothers who has a long history of truancy. He is about average in height and weight for his age. He is not very interested in school subjects. PE is his favourite. All his academic skills are weak. He reads if essential, does not like doing number work, sits placidly through most lessons.

In school he has a few close friends. Boys seem to like him for his physical prowess. If a ball goes on the roof or over the fence it is usually Peter who goes to get it, as long as no adult is watching.

The school staff are concerned about Peter. He is not doing very well. Yet there appears to be no obvious reason for his low academic attainment. He seems happy enough; he has a group of friends; he does not cause trouble. He is just not very motivated to learn. School seems like a place that he knows he has to go to every day. Not a place that offers him much excitement or interest – with the exception of games.

David – A boy with SLD

David is 13 years old. He is a stocky boy and is slightly overweight.
He wears glasses all the time. He dresses smart-casual and takes an
interest in his clothes. He lives with his Mum, Dad and two older
sisters in a village. He is much loved by all his family.

He is a very cheerful person. He laughs a lot and seems to enjoy life.
He likes being with people. At school he is popular with other pupils
and with adults. He is polite and considerate of others.

David can dress himself, but it takes a long time. Buttons present him
with serious difficulty. Left alone, and given time, he can cope with most
of them. He cannot tie shoelaces yet so often wears shoes with velcro
fastenings. He washes, toilets and feeds himself. He usually loves his food.

Although rather overweight, David is a very active boy. He enjoys
swimming, playing football, chasing about, riding a trike, camping,
going to a weekly youth club for people with special needs. He shouts,
cheers and laughs a lot. He does most things with tremendous
enthusiasm. He does not play in the village unless an adult is nearby.
He has very little understanding of traffic and the danger of roads.
Most of his life he is shadowed by an adult.

Verbal communication is a bit of a problem for him. His articulation
of words is not always clear. Words with two syllables or more are
difficult for him to say clearly. He has speech therapy sessions at
school. He can put together sentences with four or five words. He
backs up his spoken communication with Makaton – a popular form
of hand-signing for children who have communication problems. He
is very good at that.

Academically, David has serious difficulties. He reads one or two short
words. He can copy simple words. He can count up to four. In
general he prefers the more active, practical aspects of school – PE,
music, technology, science.

David is a delightful person. Always popular, generally enthusiastic, he
enjoys life enormously. His academic development will always be very
limited.

David has Down's syndrome. He was formally assessed by the local education authority (LEA). He has a statement of SEN. Amongst other things, the statement recommended speech therapy and placement in a special school. David attends a LEA day school for pupils with severe learning difficulties.

Richard – A boy with SLD

Sixteen-year-old Richard is tall and slim with a mass of curly, black hair. He stands very erect. He is a fine-looking young man with a steady gaze. He appears to be calm most of the time, watching things going on around him with an apparent lack of involvement or concern.

He takes little interest in physical activities. In a way this is a pity because he has some very well-developed skills. He can catch and throw a ball with great accuracy. Give him a large ball and basketball net and he will score baskets over and over; he never seems to tire of the activity and will go on until somebody distracts his attention.

He runs with a long, lolloping stride. If excited he will break into a fast skip rather than a run. At the same time he will start shouting, as if encouraging himself. 'Keep going! Keep going! Keep going!' Over and over, faster and faster he shouts as he gathers speed.

Richard is an only child. His mother adores him and is just a little over-protective. His father is also fond of him but is more willing to allow him to explore activities – under supervision. For example, Richard had the chance to go camping with a school group. His mother was terribly anxious about his going. His father accepted it as a perfectly reasonable activity for him to take part in.

In general Richard keeps himself to himself. He takes little notice of other people, even his parents. If visitors come to the house he takes no notice of them. His mother always tells him to say 'hello'. This he does in a flat voice that suggests a total lack of interest. He never makes conversation with the visitor.

Left to his own devices, he may stand staring out of the window of the neat family home for long periods of time. He may set about stacking playing cards into a tower. If the tower falls, as it usually does, he patiently sets about building it again. Over and over he will do this. He seems to prefer being alone rather than mixing with other people.

Whilst Richard seems to be calm, self-contained and even rather remote there are occasions when he gets very excited and agitated. For example, if his father asks him to help with the washing up, Richard will get terribly agitated. 'Don't like it! Don't like it!' He repeats this over and over. It is not just a simple unwillingness to help. There is a sense of panic in his voice. The more his father insists, the more agitated Richard becomes. If the interaction continues then he will start jumping up and down, flapping his hands. It seems that there is something deeply upsetting for him in the activity of washing up. If pushed too far he can become aggressive. His aggression is like that of a young child – pinching, poking with a finger, play-punching. His anger is very real.

Richard likes certain foods and totally rejects others. At home, he must sit at the same place for every meal – on the left side of the table with his back to the window. Should he ever be asked to sit in a different place he becomes dreadfully agitated. His parents have come to terms with this and rarely ask him to sit in anything other than 'Richard's place'.

He is most relaxed when foods are familiar to him, when everything on the table is tidily in place. If his cup and saucer are not in place he gets bothered. He really does like the security of having everything in its right place.

He washes, dresses, toilets without difficulties. He has not developed great sensitivity about appropriate clothes to wear. He will put on shorts and a t-shirt on a cold, winter day and fail to notice that these are inappropriate. Equally, he will wear an overcoat in the hottest weather if allowed to do so. As a result of this lack of awareness, his mother has to organise his clothes every morning.

Richard speaks clearly. He often repeats the words people say to him. If somebody says, 'Would you like an ice-cream?' he may parrot the sentence back. This can puzzle people who do not know him. If he does something which he knows he should not do, he may shout,

'Richard, stop it! Naughty!' He never opens a conversation. In truth, he does not really have conversations. He repeats sentences, responds rather mechanically to requests and addresses himself as if talking to another person.

Out and about in the suburb where he lives, Richard shows good sense of traffic. He can use road crossings correctly. However, he is not entirely predictable in his behaviour. It is difficult to know what might upset him. One day, he was walking along a street when he noticed a cat sitting by a garden gate. This threw him into a panic. He jumped sideways into the road. Fortunately no vehicle was coming. This kind of unpredictability of response means that his mother is not comfortable about letting him out of her sight.

In shops he will pick up any item he fancies and put it in his pocket. This makes shopping trips an ordeal for his mother and father. They have to examine his pockets at the check-out on every trip. Whilst he can then tell himself off, the distinction between right and wrong does not seem to stick in his mind.

As for academic work, Richard does not achieve at a level anywhere near that of his peers. He can read simple books but shows little understanding of the words. He can copy words in print but, again, shows little understanding. He likes counting . . . on and on until asked to stop.

Whilst he attends a special school, Richard goes one afternoon a week to the local comprehensive with a learning support assistant. There he joins a music class. He likes listening to music. He can play simple tunes on a recorder. Needless to say, he has nothing to do with other pupils at the school although the assistant tries hard to prompt interactions. Unfortunately, the other pupils seem to have little time for him.

Richard has a statement of SEN. He has had the statement for several years. His condition was diagnosed when he was five. He has autism. He has been at the same special school for children with severe learning difficulties ever since he was three.

When he leaves the school his parents hope that he will live in a community home.

Karen – A girl with PMLD

Karen is 14. She is a tall, good-looking young woman with short black hair. She is very well built and very strong. She is forever running about, kicking objects, throwing anything that she can get her hands on. She is very physical. Take her for a walk and she seems to be tireless. Take her swimming and she will jump into the deep end, climb the boards to jump off, thrash about with an imprecisely defined style but still make fast progress through the water.

She has one brother, older than her by two years. Her mother and father are travellers. They spend most of their time in their caravan on the travellers' site on the outskirts of a town.

Karen is a very likeable person. She can be very affectionate, coming up to people she knows well and kissing them. At other times she can turn her fury on the same person and become a kicking, spitting, screaming and punching whirlwind.

Her behaviour is not easy to predict. She may be sitting quietly one minute, then spring into action. People who know her get used to the unpredictability, though living with her is not easy.

With regard to self-help skills Karen has only very limited achievements. She cannot use a knife and fork, preferring to eat with her fingers. If pressed, she will use a spoon. She drinks from a cup with a spout. Dressing, toileting, washing all require much assistance. Karen seems to have abundant energy and lying down to sleep is of little interest to her. She usually wakes very early and shouts.

Communicating with other people is immensely difficult for Karen. She has no speech. She can shout and shriek but not articulate any words at all. She points at things if she wants them or simply picks them up. She does not know any sign language. It is impossible to know what concepts she understands, if any. She relies very heavily on vision and hearing to get around in the world. Her emotional responses are powerful.

Karen has to be watched and accompanied all the time. She very rarely leaves the caravan site. She has no understanding of traffic and would launch herself into the road without a thought.

Karen goes to a day school for children who have SLD and PMLD. It is quite common for both 'groups' to be educated in the same school. She is in a class for six pupils, boys and girls. One of the real problems with children such as Karen is finding the appropriate school that can meet their needs, without interfering in the education of the other pupils. Karen is rather disruptive and presents what is now known as 'challenging behaviour'.

Academically, Karen achieves very, very little. She does take part in National Curriculum subjects. Participation is limited mostly to being present in the class, watching and listening. She cannot write, read or count. Just what she understands of the world around her is impossible to say. Certainly, she does not seem to understand very much.

Karen has been examined and tested by many professionals. There is no clear, simple diagnosis. She has a range of disabilities – inability to communicate being perhaps the most serious. Her cognitive skills are extremely limited. She has a statement of SEN.

As Karen is getting older and stronger, she is becoming more difficult for her family and the school to manage. Her statement of SEN has always suggested that a day school would be appropriate for her. Now, there is an increasing feeling that soon she will probably be better placed in a residential school.

Specific learning difficulties

There are some children who have a learning difficulty in specific subjects of the curriculum. In particular, the difficulty seems to be in the key skills of reading, writing, spelling. This cluster of difficulties is usually referred to as dyslexia. This word means 'difficulty with words'.

There are many other words used to describe this condition and variations of it. The two main conditions are:

- acquired dyslexia: this occurs in adults, usually as the result of an accident
- developmental dyslexia: this occurs in children. The cause is unknown.

For our purposes we can stay with the one general word, dyslexia. If you are particularly interested in understanding the subtle variations in dyslexia then you need to consult a specialist book (see Further Reading).

There is one very puzzling thing about dyslexia. Children who have the condition are often achieving well in other areas of the curriculum. It is only in reading, writing and spelling that they have serious problems. They may be good at speaking and listening, for example, but achieve well below what you would expect in reading, writing and spelling.

One outcome of dyslexia is a high level of frustration for the pupil. This, in turn, can lead to emotional and behavioural difficulties, which can cause much unhappiness and distress for the pupil. It is estimated that 4% of children have dyslexia. Of these, the great majority are boys in the ratio of 4:1 to girls.

Some pupils also have significant difficulty with number work. In particular they have problems with counting, addition and subtraction and reciting tables.

There are numerous books written about dyslexia. It is therefore rather surprising to know that some LEAs do not acknowledge such a condition. Maybe they are just having difficulty with words!

Mark – A boy who has dyslexia

Mark is nine years old. He is about average in height and quite wiry. He has dark hair which is cut short. He is very lively. He is one of those boys who does not walk anywhere if he can possibly help it. He prefers to run. He enjoys many sports: football, cricket, athletics and swimming.

Mark has a younger brother, Paul, who is six. They live with their mother and father in a comfortable terraced house in a large town. The family are close-knit. Mark's father is a solicitor and his mother used to be a primary school teacher. They have a large garden where Mark and Paul play together. They are good friends though, like most brothers, they do have the occasional squabble.

Both boys go to a local primary school. Mark is well liked by other children. He plays in a school football team, belongs to an after-school chess club and is learning to play the recorder.

Overall, he enjoys going to school. He is a hard worker. However, his class teacher is becoming concerned about his progress, especially in reading, writing and number.

The picture that is emerging is a familiar one for the teacher. Over many years she has taught a handful of children who have been rather like Mark. Pupils who are generally able in their work, sociable and doing well in a wide range of activities. But not in the basic skills of reading and writing. And in Mark's case, number.

Mark is becoming increasingly aware of his difficulties. His level of spelling is not good. As a result his written work does not truly reflect his verbal ability. He talks well and can make good contributions to discussions. It is when he has to write things down that he gets into difficulty. He tries to avoid situations where he has to write. His reading is far below the level one might expect from him. In number work, he struggles with sequencing and learning tables.

What the teacher has noticed is that Mark is becoming increasingly angry with himself. He does not understand why he is having such difficulties. It is all very frustrating for him. He seems to know that he is a bright boy. And yet he is slipping backwards.

Mark is displaying some of the characteristics of a pupil with dyslexia. His class teacher has talked with the school's SEN co-ordinator (SENCo). A closer examination is to be made. If considered appropriate he will be referred to an educational psychologist for assessment. Steps can then be taken to help Mark.

If, after that, Mark's difficulties continue to be significant then it may be necessary for a statutory assessment to be made by the LEA.

Emotional and behavioural difficulties

Children who have emotional and behavioural difficulties (known as EBD) often fail to achieve their potential in academic terms. Their emotional problems get in the way of academic achievement. The emotional problems may become apparent from the child's behaviour. It is important to note that whilst some pupils may become disruptive, there are many others who do not.

The range of EBD is considerable. Many authors have drawn up definitions and classification systems to help understanding. In broad terms we can say that a child's behaviour will give an indication of an underlying emotional problem. There are those children whose problems have an effect on themselves; and there are others whose problems are shown by the way they interact with other people.

Here are a few of the possible symptoms of emotional problems:

- obsessions
- withdrawal from social interactions
- apathy – showing little interest in school

- tempter tantrums
- bullying
- eating disorders
- phobias
- stealing
- lying
- vandalism
- truancy.

Staff working in schools see the symptoms. They then have to try to understand the cause or causes of the symptoms. Very often they can do little about the causes. This can be frustrating. Also the staff may face a dilemma. Should they focus on the lack of educational achievement or on the EBD? Sometimes it is a chicken and egg situation – which creates which? As so often happens, a compromise is the practical answer.

Gilly – A girl with learning difficulties and EBD

Gilly is ten years of age. She is short and very strong. She has long fair hair. Often she has a cold and her nose is regularly red and sore.

Gilly is very energetic. She rarely walks anywhere unless an adult restrains her. She charges about rather than runs. Left alone she will climb on to walls, over fences, up trees. She seems to have little sense of danger. She enjoys ball games of a very simple kind. She plays football, or rather kicks a ball and then charges after it. The rules of football are too difficult for her to understand. She is a strong swimmer. She can jump into the deep end of the local pool from the springboard. This she will do over and over again.

Gilly has two older brothers, one 12 and the other 16. They encourage her tomboy ways. Her mother is very caring and gives Gilly much of her time. Her father is a long-distance driver and away from home quite a lot. The family live in a cul-de-sac on a local authority estate in a small village. The nearest town is about 15 miles away.

Gilly is a friendly girl. Indeed, her mother worries because Gilly will talk to anybody. She has no fear of people. In the village, where she is well known, Gilly will shout 'hello' to any man, woman or child she sees. If she meets a person with a dog she will run up to the dog, crouch down, talk to it, pat it. She cannot understand that a dog might be aggressive.

When she is alone Gilly sings to herself. She is not entirely in tune but she enjoys singing nursery rhymes and has a go at current pop songs. She has a cassette player in her bedroom and playing pop music is one of her great pleasures. She also watches the television – family-type programmes engage her attention.

At meal times Gilly eats steadily. She is not too fussed if food falls off her plate or on to the floor. She has a good appetite and will keep eating until her mother stops her. She prefers soft foods. She steers clear of hard fruits such as apples and pears. She seems to find these hard to bite into and chew.

She can wash, shower and dry herself. When it comes to cleaning her teeth she spends more time chewing the brush than actually brushing her teeth. Getting her into bed is a daily challenge for her mother. In the holidays she will stay up late and fall asleep in a chair rather than be isolated in her small bedroom.

Gilly dresses slowly. She does not yet seem to understand when a t-shirt or sweater is on inside out. Sometimes she puts clothes on back-to-front. She cannot tie her shoelaces.

Whilst she enjoys meeting all sorts of people, Gilly's spoken language is not always easy to understand. She talks fast. Her articulation is not always clear. As a result she gets frustrated at times when people do not understand her. Then her normal placid manner changes and she gets angry. She will repeat words over and over, louder and louder. Sometimes she works herself into a real temper. She throws anything she can lay her hands on. She kicks. Such tantrums usually end in tears.

Gilly is never allowed out alone. She goes out with her brothers from time to time. They seem to be happy with her but there are many times when they do not want her around. She seems to have no friends in the village. As a result, Gilly plays a lot in the small garden and waits for her mother to take her to a nearby park or to the shops. In the park Gilly goes on the swings and other apparatus. She is very happy there.

Gilly goes to the small village primary school. She really enjoys going to school. Probably she likes being with the other children. She has a learning support assistant with her some of the week. She takes part in subjects of the National Curriculum to the extent that her ability permits. Her academic attainment is far below that of her peers. She cannot read, cannot write words. She can count by rote up to ten. She does not understand number yet. She will sit still and listen to stories but, from the questioning, it is evident that she understands very little.

In the playground she charges about. The other children seem to be intimidated by her. She tries to join in the games that the girls play but fails to understand the rules. If excluded she may be aggressive. Or again, she may go off and sit alone in a corner of the playground.

Gilly has no clear medical diagnosis. Her cognitive skills appear to be limited. She has problems with communication. She has been assessed and now has a statement of SEN.

There was talk of sending her to a special school. Her parents wanted her to be a part of the local community. The primary school staff were willing to keep her on their roll. When the time for transfer to secondary school arrives it may well be necessary to rethink Gilly's placement.

Physical disabilities

A physical impairment may lead to a physical disability. The impairment may have a congenital origin, that is to say the child was born with a particular condition; or it may be the result of accident or illness. The physical disability may be of short or long duration. It may be mild or severe.

Some children may have other impairments as well. Cerebral palsy, for example, may lead to sensory impairment, learning difficulties, speech and language difficulties, as well as motor impairment. Children with multiple impairment will have very complex needs.

That said, it is important to remember that a child with a physical disability may be doing excellent academic work. His special needs may be focused more on problems of access: how to move around a school site in a wheelchair; how to get to the third floor of a building if there is no lift; how to get into the school swimming pool if there is no hoist.

Depending on the nature of his disability he may need more or less support from either a teacher or learning support assistant. There may be some subjects of the curriculum where he will need assistance, such as PE. There may be others where it may be necessary to make adaptations to equipment, for example in technology or computer work.

Nowadays, with goodwill, enthusiasm and adequate resources, it should be possible to meet most of the SEN of pupils with physical disabilities in mainstream schools. Many LEAs have closed schools that were specifically for children with physical disabilities. Those children who have multiple impairment are usually educated in special schools.

Philip – A boy with a physical disability

Philip is slightly built. He looks younger than his age, which is nine. He has fair hair and wears glasses. He has cerebral palsy. He cannot walk. He is unable to support his weight on his legs and spends most of his day in an electrically powered wheelchair. He seems to enjoy riding in the chair and is very skilful at negotiating obstacles.

There are five children in Philip's family. He is the fourth. He has three sisters and one brother. His mother and father run a guesthouse which caters mostly for tourists. They have a specially adapted vehicle with a ramp so that Philip can stay in his wheelchair when the family go out.

Philip likes sport. He belongs to a swimming club and goes to sessions every week with his father. Occasionally he goes to watch the local football team, again with his father.

He is a very cheerful, chirpy boy. He laughs a lot and enjoys practical jokes. Family life is full of excitement for him. His brothers and sisters play with him, take him out and about. Visitors to the guesthouse often meet him. He enjoys talking to them and finding out where they are from and what they do. His is very inquisitive about people.

He eats and drinks unaided. He needs help with dressing though he has firm ideas about what he wants to wear. He likes bright-coloured clothes. He has to be helped to get in the bath but once in it he can wash himself. The bathroom has modifications that help him to stand, to use the toilet and to be fairly independent.

The large family house is on a busy city road. As Philip is becoming more independent his parents have continually adapted their home to accommodate him. There are ramps, wider doors as necessary, electronic gadgets. He has his bedroom on the ground floor where he has his own computer. Not that he spends too much time in there alone. He seems to prefer being with the family.

The large garden has smooth winding paths that provide him with a circuit to travel around. He refers to it as his Formula One circuit. He likes driving round it as fast as possible. It gives him a great thrill to hear his mother getting worried about this. He did tip out of his wheelchair once and grazed his arm.

Philip is a real chatterbox. He keeps up a steady flow of conversation. He will talk about anything anybody brings up. Sport, pop music, TV programmes, computer games . . . he rattles away, laughing and joking as he goes.

So far, he does not go out on his own. He is allowed to sit outside the house on the pavement to watch the world go by. If he wants to go any further then he has to be accompanied. Philip's parents see the day soon when they will be happy enough for him to drive off in his wheelchair without adult supervision. They assume too that as an adult he will probably have his own car. They are keen to encourage as much mobility as they can for him.

Philip attends the local primary school, where he does well. Part of the week he is aided by a learning support assistant. She provides physical support rather than academic support. He is doing well academically, working within the appropriate level for the majority of subjects. He is particularly good at maths. This gains him some respect from other children in his class.

He is well liked by the children and staff. He has some physiotherapy at the school. A programme of exercises was created by a paediatric physiotherapist. This set of exercises for his legs and hips is delivered by the learning support assistant under the regular supervision of the physiotherapist.

Philip has a statement of SEN. So far there has been no suggestion that he should attend anything other than a mainstream school. That pleases him and his family. He is doing well academically, has many friends and enjoys participation in the life of the community. All being well, he will move on to the local comprehensive school with his friends when he is 11.

Sensory impairment: hearing difficulties

There is a wide range of hearing impairment in children. There are those children who have a mild hearing loss and can manage in mainstream school unaided; there are those who, with appropriate resources, can cope with mainstream school; and there is a small minority of children who may need specialist provision that can only be provided in a special school.

Some children may have temporary hearing loss, especially in the primary years. 'Glue ear', as it is known, is fairly common. Permanent hearing loss, especially if severe, can lead to significant communication difficulties for a child. Then there is the risk that the child may develop emotional and behavioural problems through becoming frustrated in attempts to communicate.

The development of language and communication skills can be seriously affected if a child's hearing impairment is not recognised. Early diagnosis is the key to success in meeting the needs of children with serious hearing loss.

Some children learn signing to communicate. The use of signing often creates debate with people taking positions as follows:

- for signing: signing provides a child with a tool for communication
- questioning signing: if learned as an exclusive way of communicating, signing restricts a child's interactions to communication with other signers.

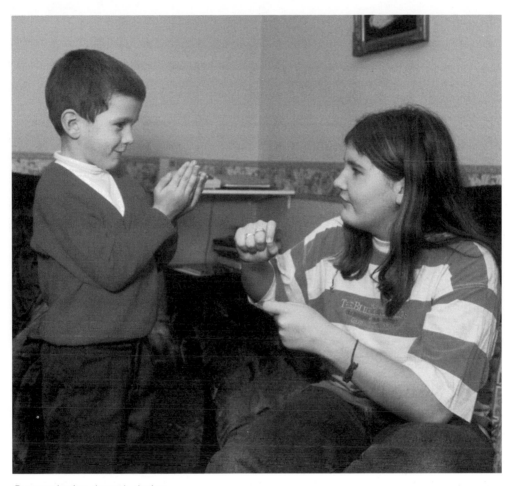

Communication through signing

Over the past 30 years there has been a tremendous shift in the education of children with hearing impairment. Most are now educated in mainstream schools. From my own experience, I can recall teaching in a residential school for 'The Deaf', as they were known, in the 1960s. Looking back, it seems extraordinary that some of the children there were excluded from mainstream. They had hearing impairment but, with hearing aids – even as they were then – the children could probably have managed in mainstream. It emphasises the change in attitude that has occurred.

Mary – A girl with a hearing impairment

Mary is eight. She is physically rather small. She is quiet and may give the impression of being withdrawn. She has one brother, who is 12. The family live in a suburban street not far from the primary school that Mary attends.

In most respects she is doing perfectly well at school. She does have a hearing loss. This was diagnosed before she started school. She now wears a small hearing aid which, in broad terms, increases the volume of sounds. With this aid, she seems to hear very well. There are times when she removes the aid. Then, she struggles to hear all the sounds of speech.

Her class teacher knows about Mary's hearing loss and the possibility that she may not always hear and, therefore, not understand. She takes care to position Mary at the front of the class. From time to time the teacher makes a particular check on Mary's understanding.

The other pupils in the class know that she wears a hearing aid. They do not seem to take any notice of it. Mary's speech is only slightly distorted. It is important that Mary uses the hearing aid. Without it, she would probably drift behind the other children in her class.

There is a Hearing Impairment Service in the county. A specialist teacher visits Mary's school on a regular basis. She discusses Mary's progress with the teacher. She looks over Mary's work and maintains a good relationship with her. Should there be any worries or problems associated with Mary's progress then the specialist teacher can make appropriate recommendations. She also meets Mary's parents and discusses progress with them.

With careful monitoring from the Hearing Impairment Service and the sensitive support of her teachers, Mary should be able to cope with her hearing impairment. This means that she should be able to move to the local comprehensive school in due course.

Sensory impairment: visual difficulties

Visual impairment can very considerably in its severity and in the degree of disability it causes. The range spans minor visual impairment, partial sightedness and blindness. These are not clear-cut categories as you will understand.

Until quite recently, blind children and many of those who are partially sighted were automatically placed in special schools. There has been a steady move away from this approach. If a LEA has a well-resourced support service then both partially sighted and blind children may be educated in mainstream schools.

One important fact to note is that something like 50% of the total number of children who have visual impairment also have SLD or PMLD. The majority of these children are educated in special schools.

Paul – A boy with visual impairment

Paul is eight years old. He is stocky in build, has fair hair and is slightly plump. He is partially sighted. In spite of this, he is very confident in physical activities. He particularly enjoys swimming and goes to the local pool with his older brother some Sunday mornings. He likes to play snooker and has a small table in his bedroom. At school, he is a member of a trampoline club.

His father is a farmer. The family live in the farmhouse which is set well back from the road. Paul can move around the farm without assistance. He enjoys riding on the tractor with his father. They have a dog, a collie, and Paul likes to take her out to the fields. There is a river at the edge of one field. Paul's parents have told him not to go there on his own.

Paul goes to his local primary school. This is a small school in a village. Fortunately, it is a modern school with well-lit corridors, bright coloured walls and level paths. He has little difficulty moving around the site.

He is very popular with his peers. He is cheerful and has a good sense of humour. They all know that he cannot see particularly well. It would be easy for them to take advantage of him – pushing ahead of him in queues, for example. The fact is, they are usually very thoughtful and if he needs help they will give it.

As a result of his statement of SEN, Paul has a learning support assistant with him for a number of hours during the week. With her support, he is able to keep up with the work. A specialist teacher from the Visual Impairment Services visits Paul in his school. She keeps a close watch on his progress and discusses matters with his class teacher. They agree that he is doing well academically.

In general terms, Paul's development is much the same as his peers. He can shower himself, dress and generally look after himself. He can negotiate road crossings, but he has to be extremely careful. His parents are keen to ensure that he develops as much independence as possible. To this end, they take him out and about whenever they can. He likes going to the shops in the nearby town, or to the beach which is just over an hour away by car. Paul has told his parents that he would like to learn to ride a bike. This is something that they have not yet agreed to. They are concerned that he will not be able to cope with traffic.

Paul has a number of friends in the village. Some visit him at the farm. They like to explore the old buildings with Paul and then have tea in the big kitchen.

All being well, Paul will continue his education in mainstream schools with appropriate support.

Speech and language difficulties

Speech and language difficulties can cause serious problems. They can make it difficult for a child to progress with learning. They can lead to frustration, especially if communication with other people is difficult. Anxiety about school can develop. Failing performance, frustration and anxiety can easily lead to behavioural problems.

There is a wide range of speech and language difficulties. They can be considered from a medical or linguistic angle.

The **medical approach** focuses on the causes of speech and language problems, such as hearing loss, brain damage, cleft palate.

In the **linguistic approach**, the focus is on the nature of the child's difficulties in speech and language rather than on the causes. There is careful analysis of how a child uses speech and language: both expressive and receptive. They way in which a child puts words together to make sentences is also carefully analysed.

There are a number of children who have what are known as secondary language impairments. As you will realise, any child with a serious hearing loss or learning difficulties that are either severe or profound and multiple may also have speech and language difficulties.

George – A boy with speech and language difficulties

George is an only child who is 13 years old. He is tall and slim with light brown hair. He has to wear glasses all the time. He is a good runner and is very well co-ordinated in the ball skills of catching and throwing. Oddly, he is not too good at kicking a ball in spite of his enthusiasm for football. He supports Manchester United though he lives nowhere near the Lancashire city and has never seen the team play other than on TV.

His mother and father dote on him. To them he can do no wrong. This is a pity for George because it means that he thinks he can do as he pleases all the time. If, as sometimes does happen, his parents tell him to do something that he does not want to do, he can dig in his heels and resist.

For example, they might say, 'George, time for bed!' If he does not want to go to bed then he will get in a foul temper. He can really go berserk, kicking, throwing things about the room, swearing and shouting.

Language presents George with problems. Not that it is immediately apparent. He is very chatty. He laughs. He asks questions. But when you pay close attention to his language you realise that it does not always make sense. For example, there are some words that he obviously does not understand. 'My Dad bought me a pair of football boots tomorrow,' he might say. Or he might ask a teacher, 'What's your Dad doing yesterday?' He often gets sentences nearly, but not quite, right. He cannot quite organise his words.

George goes to the local comprehensive school. He is a bit of a loner. Other boys rather make fun of him. They have noticed his curious speech. Also, after PE lessons, they have seen that he has trouble dressing and tying shoelaces. If they taunt him he can fly into a temper.

George spends most of his spare time on his own at home. He has little to do with other boys. He either watches TV or plays with the computer his parents have installed in his bedroom.

George does not have a statement of special educational needs at present. However, he is on the school SEN register. The Special Educational Needs Co-ordinator is aware of his difficulties and keeps a close watch on him.

Medical conditions

There are many medical conditions that can lead to learning difficulties. Some of the more common ones are: heart disease, cancers, epilepsy, cystic fibrosis, diabetes and asthma. As you will understand, the degree of severity of these medical conditions may vary considerably.

The learning difficulties will arise for different reasons:

- a child may have to spend a long period of time in hospital
- he may have to visit hospital on a regular basis over a number of years
- he may be on medication that has an impact on learning ability
- his physical condition may deteriorate over time
- there may be the added complication of emotional problems.

Whether a child will attend mainstream or special school depends very much on the nature and severity of his condition and the facilities available to meet his needs.

Helen – A girl who has epilepsy

Helen is 15. She is tall and elegant with short dark hair. She is a lively person with a bubbly personality. She enjoys a number of sports including athletics and hockey. She has played hockey for the school team. She always takes an active part in school sports days.

Helen has two brothers, both younger. Her parents are very caring and show a lot of interest in the education and welfare of their children.

Helen goes to the local comprehensive school. There, she is popular and has a wide circle of friends. She lives only a short distance from the school, so she usually walks there with friends. Her academic work is satisfactory. She did go through some difficult times, especially in the primary school.

It was in the primary years that her epilepsy became known. She had some seizures. This caused both her and her family much distress. She was put on medication. One of the side-effects of the medication was to make Helen drowsy. This made concentration a problem and her academic work suffered. Fortunately, the school was able to provide her with extra support.

Now a comfortable balance has been achieved. Helen's medication seems to be just right. She no longer has a problem with drowsiness and can take part in all the school activities.

Looking ahead, Helen is hoping to go to the local FE college when she is 16. She is interested in training for a career in a caring profession. Ideally, she wants to work with children with special needs. She is not yet sure whether that will be possible.

ACTIVITIES and QUESTIONS

1 Think back to your secondary school and then to your primary school. Were there any pupils who had SEN? How did you feel about them? Discuss your experience with others in your group.
2 If you are now at a FE or HE college, do the same exercise again. In what ways are students with SEN integrated into the life of the college? Could things be better? If so, in what ways?

3   Discuss some of the problems that can arise in putting children into specific categories of learning difficulty or impairment.

4   With other students, discuss some of the daily difficulties involved in having a visual impairment.

5   Repeat the previous activity, but this time experiencing 'having a hearing impairment'.

6   Do a tour of your college. How would students with SEN access the site? (E.g. student in wheelchair, student with V.I. or H.I.)?

7   Choose one area of learning difficulty or impairment that particularly interests you. Explore it in some depth. Create a small booklet that highlights the difficulties of your chosen area and include any suggestions you may have to make life easier for someone with that particular SEN.

8   Dyslexia is a controversial subject. Why do some people say there is no such condition? Discuss this in your group.

9   Find out if there are any clubs in your area for people with learning difficulties or impairments. Create a wall display about the clubs, or visit a club and write up an account of the experience. Share your findings with other students.

3

Conditions That May Lead to Learning Difficulties

As you may imagine there are hundreds, if not thousands, of conditions that may lead to learning difficulties for children. It is helpful to think of these conditions as being in two broad groups – internal and external:

- internal conditions are to do with the body and mind of the child – such things as impairment of limbs, disease, deficiencies or damage to organs of the body, emotional and psychological disorders
- external conditions refer to the quality of the environment in which a child grows up, the family, the school he attends and the society in which he lives.

One of the most comprehensive listings of conditions must be *The CAF Directory of Specific Conditions and Rare Syndromes*. The directory is published by an organisation called Contact a Family, hence CAF. The purpose of the organisation is to provide a range of services for families with a child who has any type of disability or special need. It comes in a loose-leaf format and is regularly updated. This publication is a mine of information and should be on the library shelves of any college where students are studying special needs.

This chapter includes basic information about some of the more common conditions that may lead to learning difficulties. If you need further details then I suggest you refer to *The CAF Directory*. There you will find information about hundreds of services, support groups, associations and societies. In Appendix 2 of this book you will find contact addresses for some of the major organisations.

Conditions

Here, then, in alphabetical order are some of the conditions that may lead to learning difficulties.

Asperger syndrome

This is a variation of autism. The name comes from Hans Asperger who worked in Vienna and wrote about the disorder in 1944. As suggested in the section on autism, there is an extended range of symptoms of autism and the degree of severity of those symptoms. Asperger syndrome refers to those autistic children who are usually more academically able. They still show many of the characteristics of autism. However, they usually have language, can hold a conversation, are not quite so detached from the world around them and can make good academic progress.

Asthma

In asthma the airways become blocked causing difficulty in breathing. Some children are allergic to substances such as pollen, specific foods and dust, all of which could cause an asthma attack. Exercise, smoke and infection may also cause an attack. The severity of asthma varies from child to child. About 10% of all children have some degree of asthma. It is a condition that can be life threatening.

Children may be on preventative medication or medication to relieve symptoms during an attack. Usually children who have asthma carry an inhaler which they learn to use as and when necessary. It is important to ensure that children with asthma do carry their inhaler with them around the school and when they leave the premises.

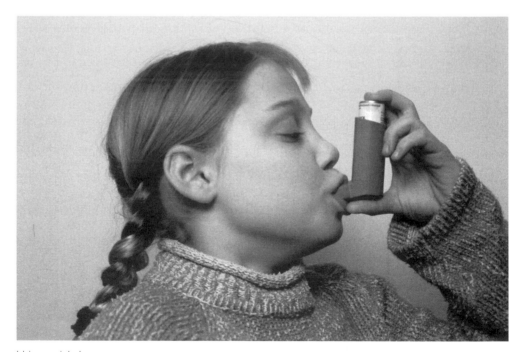

Using an inhaler

In itself asthma does not lead to learning difficulties. It is absence from school that may leave gaps in learning. Also, some pupils will only participate in physical activities in a limited way.

Attention Deficit Hyperactivity Disorder

This name is rather a mouthful. The condition is usually referred to as ADHD. There are a number of symptoms. A child must show several of them for at least six months before a diagnosis can be made.

In comparison with his peers a child with ADHD may show some of the following characteristics:

- difficulty in paying attention
- impulsive behaviour
- hyperactivity
- excessive talking
- unawareness of danger.

As you will understand, the condition can make learning very difficult. In recent years there has been considerable interest in the condition. Whereas some years ago a pupil may have been labelled 'naughty', there is now more widespread understanding that, in fact, the child has a diagnosed disorder.

There is controversy about the use of medication to control the symptoms.

Autism

The name for this disorder comes from the Greek word *autos* which means 'self'. It was first described by the American Leo Kanner in 1943. Autism can affect people to varying degrees. The phrase 'Autistic Spectrum Disorder' (ASD) is used to cover the range of autism. The most important symptoms are as follows:

SOCIAL INTERACTION PROBLEMS

Children with autism do not understand social situations and how to behave in them. They will often be isolated, have little or no contact with other people and seem happiest when left alone in their own world. They seldom play with other children. Eye contact is rare. They may show complete disregard for the feelings and needs of other people.

COMMUNICATION PROBLEMS

These are closely linked to difficulties in social situations. Language may be very limited or even non-existent. In conversation a child may repeat word for word the sentence said to him. He may talk of himself in the third person, or may avoid using language and rely on simple gestures to communicate needs.

RITUALS AND INFLEXIBILITY

Because children with autism do not seem to understand the world around them they are often very anxious. Rituals help them to cope with the dreadful anxiety they can experience. They may like things to be in the same place all the time, or have an obsession with doing an activity in precisely the same way every time.

With regard to play, they often prefer very repetitive activities. A child might line up objects over and over again. They rarely take part in 'pretend' or imaginative play or group activities.

People with autism have sometimes been portrayed in firms and other media as having outstanding ability in one particular activity such as painting, playing the piano, memorising train timetables. Such people are extremely rare. Many people with autism have MLD or SLD.

Some years ago it was thought that autism was caused by poor parenting. This is not true. It is now known that the condition is organic – damage to the brain with a possible genetic link. Whilst there is no cure for autism, appropriate education can be very beneficial.

See also Asperger syndrome.

Cancers and Leukaemia

A cancer occurs when certain body cells multiply uncontrollably and create a tumour. In leukaemia, the white blood cells are affected. These cells are essential for the body's fight against infection. There are a number of types of leukaemia and various related disorders.

Treatment for cancers can lead to time off school and a low level of health. This may cause gaps in learning and the need for special support. An intensely poignant and disturbing account of a child with cancer is Dorothy Judd's book *Give Sorrow Words – working with a dying child*.

Cerebral palsy

Cerebral palsy is caused by damage to the brain during pregnancy or on delivery. The part of the brain that controls movement is affected. This may cause disability of all four limbs or any combination of them. Other areas of the brain may also be damaged. As a result, children with cerebral palsy may have a number of disabilities: motor problems, visual and hearing impairment, speech and perceptual difficulties.

The main types of cerebral palsy are:

- spasticity – muscles are contracted and very tight. Movement is jerky and uncontrolled
- athetosis – muscles are relaxed but movement of the arms and legs is uncontrolled
- ataxia – the sense of balance is affected and walking is awkward. A child may fall often.

Learning difficulties cover the spectrum from moderate to profound and multiple.

Cystic fibrosis

Cystic fibrosis is a disorder that affects the lungs and pancreas. Airways are blocked with mucus. This makes breathing difficult. The functioning of the pancreas is faulty and this can lead to digestive disorders. At present there is no cure for the condition.

Children with cystic fibrosis may be absent from school due to ill-health. This can lead to gaps in learning and the need for extra support in school.

Deaf/blind rubella

Deafblindness (loss of sight and hearing), is usually caused when rubella (german measles) is contracted by the mother early in pregnancy. This is why it is so important for schools and early years settings to notify visitors and parents if there are any cases of rubella in the establishment. Meningitis can also cause the dual impairment.

Children who have deafblindness need very specialised educational support.

Diabetes

In diabetes the body fails to regulate the amount of sugar in the blood. This is due to the low level of the hormone insulin produced by the pancreas. The condition can appear in children and young adults. Some of the signs are thirst, excessive urination, drowsiness and eventually coma.

The correct balance of sugar in the blood needs to be maintained. This is achieved through an adapted diet and the regular injection of insulin. Children learn to administer their own injections.

Children with diabetes can usually take a full part in educational activities. It is important that school staff and pupils are aware of the symptoms of the condition and the need for a correct diet and insulin.

Down's syndrome (or Down syndrome)

In 1866 Dr John Langdon Down described the condition that is known by his name. Down's syndrome arises from a genetic disorder in which the person has an extra chromosome 21. The condition is sometimes known as Trisomy 21. Increasingly, the condition is known as *Down* syndrome – no possessive. About one in 1000 babies is born with the syndrome.

There is still quite a lot of public misunderstanding about people who have Down's syndrome. They may share some physical characteristics but they are very much individuals and should be treated as such. Children with this syndrome may also have:

- hearing and visual problems
- delayed development
- heart problems at birth (40%).

They all have learning difficulties that may be moderate or severe.

Dyslexia

Dyslexia is a condition in which a child has difficulty learning to read. There may also be difficulties with spelling and writing. Dyslexia is sometimes

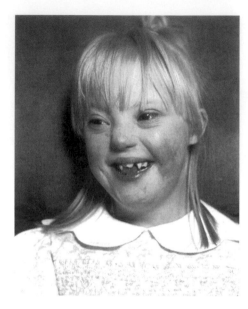

referred to as specific learning difficulties. There is no obvious reason why the child has these difficulties. He may achieve good academic standards in other areas of learning. The failure to acquire literacy skills can be puzzling.

Dyslexia has been known to exist since the late 19th century. The name derives from two Greek words and means 'difficulty with words'. It is a controversial subject and there are still people who challenge the existence of such a condition. The reality is that, whatever the disputes over theory, there are children who, inexplicably, fail to read, spell and write.

In addition to the obvious learning difficulties that the condition can create, children with dyslexia may have low self-esteem and become frustrated, angry and disruptive.

Dyspraxia

Dyspraxia is sometimes referred to as 'clumsy child syndrome' which is itself a rather clumsy description. In this condition a child has difficulty with physical movement, language development may be delayed and there may be perceptual problems.

Learning difficulties can arise, especially where fine or gross motor skills are needed.

Epilepsy

Epilepsy is a condition that is often misunderstood and feared by the public.

The vocabulary of epilepsy has changed over the years. The changes have often been introduced in order to make the condition better understood and accepted.

Epilepsy is caused by a temporary disturbance in brain function. This can lead to seizures (at one time known as 'fits' or grand mal). Seizures can be general, with whole body convulsions and unconsciousness (known as tonic clonic seizures). They can also be partial (or focal) with limited spasms; or they can be almost imperceptible with an 'absence' that lasts only a few seconds. This was previously known as petit mal.

Epilepsy is often controlled with medication. This can lead to undesirable side-effects, such as drowsiness. In school, the drowsiness can reduce the ability to concentrate.

The severity of epilepsy varies. Some children attend mainstream school without any problems. Others may have learning difficulties requiring special support.

Fragile X Syndrome

An inherited condition so named because there is a fragile site on the X chromosome. This is more common in boys than girls. Most have learning difficulties – from severe to mild; some have autistic-type behaviour.

Hearing impairment

Deafness is the major symptom of a hearing impairment. There may be a dysfunction in the ear, the nerves or the brain. The resulting deafness may be total or partial. A hearing impairment can cause problems in learning.

Heart defects

About one in 150 babies is born with some kind of heart defect. That is to say, it is congenital. Infection can cause heart defects. Some children with other syndromes, such as Down's syndrome, may also have heart problems. Surgery may be necessary.

Absence from school for treatment may have an effect on a child's academic achievement. After treatment, with appropriate management, many children with heart defects can attend mainstream school.

Muscular dystrophy

Muscular dystrophy refers to a number of conditions in which the muscles of the body waste away. The most common type is Duchenne muscular dystrophy. Only boys are affected. The muscles of the body gradually get weaker and weaker over several years. At present there is no cure for the condition.

With appropriate support a boy with Duchenne muscular dystrophy should be able to attend a mainstream school.

Poliomyelitis

Poliomyelitis, also known as infantile paralysis or just 'polio', is uncommon in the UK now thanks to vaccination. It causes paralysis of varying degrees of severity. Whilst the condition is rare now, it led to serious physical disability for many children in the 1960s. Children arriving in the UK from countries where there is no vaccination programme may have 'polio'.

The nature of a child's special needs will depend on the severity of the paralysis.

Prader-Willi syndrome

Prader-Willi syndrome was identified in 1956 by Swiss doctors Prader, Willi and Labhard. The condition is associated with a chromosome abnormality. There are a number of features including:

- hypotonia (low muscle tone)
- hypogonadism (immature development of sex organs)
- obesity which is caused by excessive over-eating
- short stature
- delays in speech and walking
- learning disability.

Children with this condition usually have MLD or SLD.

Speech and language impairment

Speech and language impairment can be caused by many factors. There are basically two kinds – primary and secondary communication disorder:

- in primary communication disorder the child's general development is normal

- secondary communication disorder occurs in combination with another condition such as cerebral palsy, chromosome defects or one of the many syndromes.

Clearly the severity of the impairment will have a direct impact on the significance of the learning difficulties.

Spina bifida

Spina bifida develops in the growing foetus, early in the pregnancy. The spinal cord develops a malformation in which some of the vertebrae fail to form properly. As a result there is a gap in the spine.

There are a number of variations in spina bifida:

- spina bifida occulta which is a very mild form
- spina bifida cystica. This is a far more serious condition. Where the gap occurs at the spine a sac develops. This sac can contain nerves and part of the spinal cord. If there is damage to these then the child may be paralysed and have loss of sensation below the level of the sac
- cranium bifida. In this condition the bones of the skull fail to develop properly. Again a sac forms which may contain part of the brain
- hydrocephalus. This condition is sometimes known as 'water on the brain' and often associated with spina bifida. There is a build-up of cerebro-spinal fluid in the brain which can cause serious damage to the brain.

Children with spina bifida may have a range of learning difficulties, both physical and intellectual.

Visual impairment

Visual impairment occurs if either the eye, nerves linking the eye with the brain, or area of the brain controlling vision are defective or damaged. Blindness, which can be total or partial, is a symptom of visual impairment. A child may be born with an impairment (congenital) or acquire an impairment during life.

The child's learning difficulties will depend very much on the severity of the impairment.

ACTIVITIES and QUESTIONS

1   Try to find a copy of the *CAF Directory* (or any other similar directory). Familiarise yourself with its contents.

2   Select some conditions that may lead to learning difficulties that interest you. Find out as much information as you can about them.

3   Watch the film/video *Rain Man* (about a man who has autism, played by Dustin Hoffman). Discuss your thoughts on autism with other students.

4   Select two or three conditions that may lead to learning difficulties. Discuss with other students how they might affect learning.

5   Choose one condition. If you had the condition, how might it affect your learning?

4

Meeting Special Educational Needs

We will now look at some of the ways of meeting children's special educational needs. First of all, we will consider approaches that are relevant to a wide range of children and young adults. Then we will look at formal educational provision from early years to further education.

Communication

We communicate with each other through our senses, cognitive skills, emotions and body language. We use speech, writing, gestures, facial expressions. Children with SEN may have serious difficulties with communication. For example, some do not hear well enough to follow speech; some cannot see well enough to read; some cannot understand language; some do not have the ability to speak.

Let's look at some of the ways devised to help communication.

Braille

Braille is a method of reading for people with visual impairment. It was named after the man who created the system.

Louis Braille, a Frenchman, went blind when he was three years old. As a teenager he was a student at the National Institute for Blind Children in Paris. There, in 1824, when he was 15 years old, he invented a way of writing text that could be read by touch.

The system uses 6 dots which are raised from the surface of the paper. They are placed in different groupings in a cell. Each grouping represents a letter of the alphabet. The reader passes his fingers lightly over the dots and reads the letters by touch.

Braille was accepted in the UK in 1932.

Makaton

Makaton is a popular communication system. It is used by a wide range of people, including those with learning difficulties, hearing impairment, autism, language disorders. It is used by children and adults.

This system was designed in 1972 by Margaret Walker, a speech therapist, working in London. Initially, she devised a form of manual signing to help deaf adults with severe learning difficulties to communicate. This pilot study proved successful and Makaton grew from there.

Today, Makaton combines manual signing with speech as an effective way of communication. Further, visual symbols have been created so that Makaton can be used for writing and public signs.

Makaton is constantly developing. It is used in a wide range of settings – education, health, social services. Training courses are provided in most parts of the UK.

Sherborne Developmental Movement

Sherborne – as this system is usually known – uses physical movement as a means of communication between people.

The approach was created by Veronica Sherborne, a teacher working in the UK. She developed her system for children with severe learning difficulties. Now, it is used with adults as well.

Sherborne uses physical movement and play-like activities. These can be enjoyable and valuable in themselves. However, the deeper value of the approach lies in the development of self-awareness and relationships between participants.

The approach is very popular in special schools and some hospital settings. Training courses are available.

Aromatherapy, Art Therapy, Music Therapy, Play Therapy, Dance Therapy

There are numerous types of therapy available. These are widely used with children who have SEN. They have many benefits but an underlying purpose in all of them is communication, in particular communication of emotions.

We have now considered just a few of the many ways of developing communication for children with SEN. Other ways of meeting special educational needs include the following:

CONDUCTIVE EDUCATION

This approach was developed in Hungary by Andras Peto. Its headquarters are at the Peto Institute in Budapest. The UK centre is in Birmingham.

Conductive Education is for children who have basic motor problems – difficulties with sitting, standing, walking, holding objects and so on. Treatment is intensive. It involves parents and is co-ordinated by one person – the conductor. Hence the name.

EQUIPMENT

Some children have special needs with regard to physical movement. There is an enormous range of equipment available to meet such needs. Manufacturers publicise their equipment in relevant magazines and at exhibitions.

As you will realise there are many other ways of meeting special educational needs. We can now consider the formal educational approaches.

Let us just recall some figures. About 20% of all children have SEN at some time or other during their school career. Of those, only 2% have a statement of SEN.

Nearly all children with SEN are educated in mainstream schools. It is very important to keep hold of this fact. It is all too easy to assume that most children with SEN are educated in special schools. They are not. Special schools cater for less than 2% of pupils who have SEN.

Another point to bear in mind is that there are many variations in provision across the UK. What is described here may not exist in your area. There may well be something similar but with different details. The bottom line is that all LEAs have an obligation to meet the needs of pupils who have SEN. How they organise that provision is up to the authority.

We shall look at provision in the following order, bearing in mind that some services will overlap or cover the entire age range:

- early years
- mainstream primary and secondary
- special schools
- independent
- FE colleges

We shall also look briefly at recreational provision for children with SEN.

Early years provision

However it is described, there will usually be some form of early years learning support service. It will probably be part of the authority's total support network for children with SEN. Here we can look at the early years provision apart. In some ways it is different from other areas of the service.

An early years support service is available for children under school age who have, or may have, SEN. Parents who are concerned about the development of their child can contact the service.

There will probably be teachers and nursery nurses working in the service. They will visit the family and start the process of assessment. The home is the main focus for this assessment. If the child goes to a playgroup, early years opportunity group or nursery then the teacher and nursery nurse may well make a visit there to observe the child.

After the assessment a decision is made as to whether the child is or is not developing normally. If the child's difficulties are not significantly greater than those of other children then that is the end of the matter. Parents will be reassured.

If help is considered necessary then the teacher and nursery nurse will establish a programme for the child. They will provide regular support to the family and monitor progress. (In Chapter 5 there is a more detailed description of an early years worker's work.)

The support service will also have strong links with other services such as the health, social and psychological services. There will be close liaison between professions to ensure that the parents and their child receive the best possible support. Where appropriate, the statementing process can be started in the early years.

Early Excellence Centres

There are a number of such centres across the UK. They provide an integrated service for young children and their parents. Education, Health and Social Services all work together. The centres are inclusive and include children with SEN.

One other specific service that the early years learning support service might offer parents is Portage.

Portage

Portage is a scheme for teaching very young children who have special needs. It is first and foremost a home-teaching scheme, though it is used in some special schools.

Before we go any further we must sort out the name. Portage is the name of a rural area in the USA. The home teaching scheme began there in the 1970s, in Wisconsin to be precise. It was set up to meet the needs of children who had learning difficulties and who lived in rural areas. The scheme became known the world over as Portage.

What makes this scheme different is that it is taken to the children in their homes. And it is delivered primarily by the parents. Portage is based on the fact that the experts on a particular child are the parents of the child.

The parents are the teachers. Of course, Portage home visitors, as they are called, work with the parents. They visit the home. With the parents they assess the child's level of development in many key areas, such as motor development, social skills, language, self-help.

The parents and home visitor agree aims and activities that might promote development. Together they design an individual programme, based on the skills steps that Portage has formulated since the 1970s.

Portage in action

Jean and Joseph have a son, Eric. When Eric was only a few weeks old he was diagnosed as having Prader-Willi syndrome. 'As soon as we found out, we decided that we would do everything possible for Eric,' explained Jean.

One of the first things she did was to get in touch with her local early years support service. 'It was agreed we should start using Portage when Eric was a few months old.'

First of all the area Portage Co-ordinator visited the family. 'She told us all about the service. She observed Eric. Together we went through a checklist to establish the level of his development in a wide range of skills and activities.' That first visit provided a baseline.

A Portage home visitor, Caroline, was appointed. She had trained and worked as a nursery nurse before joining the Portage service. She visits the family once a week.

On one such visit Jean and Caroline discuss Eric's progress: how he is progressing with rolling from back to front, how he is sitting, how he is learning to hold a cup. Eric, sitting well on the floor, plays a ball rolling game with his mother. This is a recently acquired skill. It is much enjoyed and appreciated.

'Portage has made me examine all skills very closely,' said Jean. 'You have to break even the simplest skill down into fine details.' It is this systematic, step–by–step approach that makes Portage so successful.

Now, after several months of experience, the Portage approach is built into all of Eric's learning. 'We don't have a daily Portage session,' explained Jean. 'We use the same approach for all Eric's activities.' Without the focus on detailed, tiny steps and the enthusiasm of his parents, it is possible that Eric would simply lie about and not develop at all.

'Portage has helped us to create an individual learning programme for Eric,' explained Jean. 'It's not a rigid system. We have used the approach to address Eric's special needs. It can be adapted for any child's early learning.'

Jean has her own checklist. 'We go through it from time to time. When you are with your child all the time you don't always see changes and developments. Other people notice them. By going through the checklist we can see that Eric is making progress.'

The Portage service includes activity sheets. The parents and home visitor will decide to focus on one particular skill, probably linked to the developmental checklist. 'There are also cards which provide ideas on how to teach a skill,' explained Jean.

'Once parents understand the Portage approach,' added Caroline, 'they start introducing ideas of their own on how to teach skills.' This parental input is welcomed.

A significant and unplanned aspect of the Portage service is that the home visitor can provide emotional support for a family. 'I must admit,' said Jean, 'I really do look forward to Caroline's visits. She is always positive and her support is very valuable.' Caroline will probably continue to visit Eric until he is ready to go to school full-time.

Mainstream primary and secondary provision

The 'Code of Practice ... (revised 2001), which we have often referred to, now forms the basis for provision in mainstream schools. Since 1994, all schools should have the structure in place to respond to children who have SEN.

There will be a Special Educational Needs Policy. There will also be a special educational needs co-ordinator (SENCo) (see Chapter 5 for further details about the work of a SENCo). The SENCo is the key teacher in a school where children with SEN are concerned. This teacher oversees the support that is provided for children with SEN and, where necessary, organises additional support services.

In most local authorities the SENCo will turn to some form of learning support service. The service may well include some or all of the following:

- learning support teachers/advisory teachers
- specialist services for children with hearing or visual impairment
- educational psychologists
- support centres for pupils with emotional and behavioural difficulties (EBD)
- assessment services
- careers service
- an advisory service for parents.

Learning support teachers/advisory teachers and specialist teachers for children with either hearing or visual impairment will usually have a base within their area of operation. This may be an office in an administrative building or a room in a school. From this base they travel to schools in their area. They have several functions including the following:

- to provide teaching for specific pupils
- to offer guidance to mainstream teachers
- to manage their own team of learning support assistants who may be involved in delivering programmes
- to consult with parents
- to provide reports as necessary.

There are other ways in which provision can be made in mainstream schools. A local authority may decide that certain schools in its region or city will have additional resources to meet the needs of children with a particular kind of SEN.

For example, you may find primary schools that provide special resources to meet the needs of pupils with one of the following:

- visual impairment
- hearing impairment
- speech and language difficulties
- physical disabilities.

There will usually be a secondary school with similar provision. Pupils will be able to transfer from the primary school to a suitable secondary school that is within reasonable travelling distance.

The actual provision for pupils with sensory impairment or physical disabilities can vary. There was a time when the idea of a Unit was very popular. For example, on a mainstream site you would have a 'Hearing Impaired Unit'. This would be a separate classroom, or separate building (often a Portakabin). The pupils with hearing impairment would spend much of their day learning together.

In recent years the idea of a separate Unit has lost some of its appeal. After all, it was segregated provision. Nowadays, it is more usual to include pupils with sensory impairment or physical disabilities in the mainstream classes. In that setting they will be provided with resources and learning support as required.

Accurate assessment of a child's learning difficulties is essential if the correct provision is to be made. Assessment classes, usually in a few primary schools, are for those children whose learning difficulties are not easily specified. The time spent in such a class enables staff to identify and specify the nature of the learning difficulties. That done, steps can be taken to meet the child's needs.

Assessment will also be in the hands of educational psychologists. There will always be some kind of educational psychology service in a local authority. Educational psychologists are kept busy assessing children, in particular for the statementing process. They also work with teachers and parents in matters concerning learning difficulties, emotional and behavioural problems of individual children.

Increasingly you will find mainstream staff seeking advice from staff who work in special schools. This sharing of knowledge and expertise between

Testing

people who are actually teaching and working in the schools has much to recommend it. Credibility is very high.

Take an example. A mainstream teacher has a boy with autism in her class. She has never met a child with autism before. Down the road is a special school where staff have been educating children with autism for many years. What could be more sensible than to ask staff at the special school for guidance? The mainstream teacher knows that the special school teacher will give guidance and advice based on daily experience. This form of provision may be informal. It works – and is very cost-effective.

There may well be provision for children, especially secondary pupils, who have EBD. Some authorities run small day centres that offer special tuition for such pupils.

The centres are staffed by teachers and learning support assistants with relevant expertise and experience. Pupils may attend the centre for part of the week or the whole week; short-term or long-term. The aim is to reduce the child's difficulties to a level where he can return full-time to mainstream school.

Special provision – primary and secondary

Most LEAs still have a number of special schools. These exist to educate pupils whose needs, it is judged, cannot be adequately met in a mainstream school.

A special school usually has the resources and staff to educate children who have a similar type of special need. It is this narrow focus, of course, that makes the school 'special'. In most LEAs there will be schools for children with:

- moderate learning difficulties (MLD)
- severe learning difficulties (SLD) and profound and multiple learning difficulties (PMLD)
- emotional and behavioural difficulties (EBD).

Less frequently, you might find a school that is for children with physical disabilities and/or medical problems.

You may have little or no experience of special schools. Certainly, I found that most students coming on work experience/placement in the special school where I last taught had never set foot in a special school before. Not surprisingly, some of them were anxious. Here I will try to give you some idea of what a special school might be like.

First, a few shared characteristics of special schools:

- all tend to be small compared with mainstream schools. Many will have 40–60 pupils. Others will have less; a few will have more
- class sizes are small, with about 6 to 12 pupils – maybe more in an MLD school
- teachers often have special qualifications in an area of special needs
- each class will have a teacher and one or more learning support assistants
- the age range may be from 2 to 19 years
- the atmosphere will be less formal than a mainstream school
- many of the pupils will live a considerable distance from the school and travel by taxi or a school bus
- there may be both day and residential provision. The residential provision is often five days a week, term-time only.

You will find that schools for children with MLD and schools for children with EBD are equipped in much the same way as mainstream schools. Schools for children who have SLD or PMLD may have specialised equipment and facilities. Here is one such school. We will call it Redbush School.

Redbush School

Redbush is a local authority special school for pupils with severe learning difficulties. There are also a number of pupils who have PMLD on the school roll. In all there are 60 pupils, from 2 to 19 years of age.

The single-storey building stands in a quiet road of a city suburb. The buildings are set in attractive grounds with flowerbeds, shrubbery and plenty of old trees. There is a small tarmac playground at the back of the school. In the playground there are various items of play equipment –

swings, a slide, climbing frame and playground markings. There is no playing field.

Inside the school there is a small gym which also serves as a dining hall. There are a number of small classrooms. They are furnished according to the age of the pupils. There are no desks, only tables and chairs. In some rooms there are standing frames, soft wedges for pupils to lie on, and gym mats on the floor. These mats are used for physiotherapy exercises. There is a computer in each classroom with extra equipment, such as a touch-screen and a variety of control switches. There may be a display of Makaton signs on the wall. This signing system is very popular in schools like Redbush.

THE TEACCH CLASS

One classroom is set up in a rather unusual way. This is a classroom where six children with autism are taught. In this classroom the TEACCH method is used. This is an American approach that has been very successful in the USA for over 20 years. An increasing number of schools in the UK are using the method.

TEACCH stands for The Treatment and Education of Autistic and Communication Handicapped Children. You can see why they dropped the full title.

The TEACCH approach is a response to some of the shared characteristics of children with autism. Often these children are anxious because they do not understand the environment; they cannot distinguish relevant from irrelevant data; they cannot cope with change; they prefer information presented visually.

The classroom addresses these needs. It is rather bare (reducing irrelevant data). The room is divided into areas for specific activities. Each child has his own work station, screened from others (to reduce distraction and help focus on a task). The day is carefully structured with periods of work clearly defined. Each task has a clear start and a clear end. Choice of recreation is encouraged. Teaching is either individual or in small groups.

The result of this system is a great reduction in anxiety, improved behaviour and increased learning.

That, briefly, is TEACCH. As you will realise there is more to it than this. It is a very successful system that is used for children and adults. Whilst being described here in a special school, the system can be adapted for use in a mainstream school, at home and in residential settings.

HYDROTHERAPY POOL

There is a small, heated indoor swimming pool. The pool serves both as a facility for hydrotherapy and for teaching swimming. There are a number of special features to encourage sensory stimulation: a sound system for music; a wide variety of lighting effects; smoke effects. Physiotherapy and rehabilitation programmes are delivered in the pool.

THE SENSORY ROOM

A small darkened room is called 'The Sensory Room'. In some schools it might be known as 'The Light Room'. It is for sensory stimulation or relaxation. A combination of visual, sound, tactile effects and scents can be used either to stimulate or relax children. There are coloured lights, music, attractive surfaces to touch, aromatherapy oils and moving displays. Children can interact with the equipment, controlling effects.

THE SOFT PLAY ROOM

Another larger room is known as 'The Soft Play Room'. In this room brightly coloured foam-filled equipment of different shapes and sizes is scattered about on gym mats. In here, children with movement problems can explore space and objects in safety.

REBOUND THERAPY

In the gym there is a trampoline. This is used for an activity called 'Rebound Therapy'. This form of therapy is beneficial for children who have limited movement skills and who may also lack movement confidence.

Trained members of staff work on the trampoline with individual children. The therapy aims to exercise under-developed muscles, increase confidence in movement and provide enjoyment.

VISITING THERAPISTS

A number of therapists visit the school during the week. These include:

- speech and language therapist
- physiotherapist
- occupational therapist
- music therapist
- aromatherapist.

In most instances, the therapists are employed in response to a recommendation on a child's statement. (See Chapter 5 for further details.)

In addition to these special activities in the school, the needs of pupils are met in other locations. Pupils go pony riding at a local stables through a Riding for the Disabled scheme (RDA). There are weekly trips into the community to learn such skills as road crossing, shopping, ordering and paying for a drink in a café, using a bus, finding your way around in a town. Simple as some of these may sound, there are many pupils at Redbush School who need hours and hours of practice in order to master them.

Most of the above features will be found, in some form or other, in schools for pupils who have SLD or PMLD. As you may understand, it might be difficult for every mainstream school to have this range of specialised facilities, staff and activities. This is one reason why many people insist that special schools have an important place in the whole range of educational provision for children with SEN.

Independent schools and centres

There is a long history of private education for children with SEN. Often the schools or centre are residential. Some are run by religious

organisations. Others are run by charities, such as Scope, The Royal National Institute for the Blind, Royal National Institute for the Deaf, The National Autistic Society. Each provides education for pupils with a particular range of needs.

There are also small private ventures, sometimes run by a group of people who have a shared interest in a particular learning difficulty, such as autism (e.g. Prior's Court School, Berkshire).

These private schools and centres make an important contribution to the whole educational map. Local authorities cannot always provide the appropriate education for all children within the boundaries of their authority. It is then that they turn to the private sector. The LEA will fund children to go to a special, private school if that is considered the best option.

Excellent as the provision may be, there is one possible drawback. The school or centre may be a considerable distance from the child's home. His links with family and friends may be rather restricted. However, as in all things, it is important to decide priorities. If appropriate education is given top priority then the distance from home has to be accepted.

Provision in further education

Children with SEN may leave school at 16 or stay on until they are 19. Whenever they leave school there is often a problem. Where do they go? What do they do? In particular, educational opportunities are limited.

It is an unfortunate fact that post-school provision, in terms of education, is not adequate to meet the demand. The result is that many school-leavers with SEN have to fight to get into some kind of educational establishment. Even then, they may only get part-time education at a local college of FE. Furthermore, the provision may not really address their needs.

Part of the problem is that responsibility for providing post-school provision is shared between a number of agencies: educational, health, social and employers. The Further and Higher Education Act 1992 made it clear that FE colleges had a duty to consider the requirements of students with SEN.

However, when it became apparent that the comments in this Act had not led to a substantial improvement in educational provision, a committee was set up to look into matters. This was the Tomlinson Committee.

In June 1996 the Committee published its report. It was called *Inclusive Learning*. The Report was the result of a three-year investigation into educational provision for students with learning difficulties and/or disabilities.

The idea of inclusive learning has developed with full awareness of the concept of integration. It is not the same thing. It focuses more on identifying the needs of students with SEN and then meeting those needs. In many colleges this will mean redesigning courses with the needs of those students with WEN held firmly in mind.

This is an important report. It is a blueprint for future developments in the FE world.

Unsatisfactory as the national picture may be, there are FE colleges where provision is good – even if limited. There are colleges with specifically designed vocational courses; facilities to address particular needs; necessary support services for students with hearing impairment or visual impairment.

Recreational provision

Recreation is as important for children and adults with SEN as for anybody else. Public awareness of this is increasing. This awareness has developed, in part, because of media coverage of such events as the Special Olympics, Paralympics, and the London Marathon's race for wheelchair competitors.

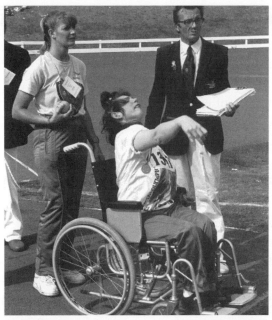

More and more people with SEN are taking part in sport

There are any number of recreational services for children with SEN. Indeed, you can probably find an organisation for just about any sporting activity. The range extends from local clubs to international organisations.

English Federation of Disability Sport (EFDS)

This is an umbrella association that co-ordinates sport for people with disabilities. There is a network of 10 regions in England, (see address list).

ACTIVITIES and QUESTIONS

1 Think back to your own primary and secondary school days. What range of provision was made for pupils with SEN? Discuss with other students.

2 Find out what kind of early years education support service is in your area.

3 What is the role of nursery nurses in early years and primary provision in your area?

4 Portage: see if you can meet a family that is using this learning scheme.

5 What are the main features of Portage?

6 What learning support service exists in your area for primary and secondary schools?

7 Describe some of the characteristics of a special school.

8 Find out what range of special schools exist in your area.

9 Contact a special school that is of particular interest to you and arrange to visit.

10 Find out what provision and courses your college offers for students with SEN. Discuss with other students.

11 TEACCH is an increasingly popular way of teaching children who have autism. Find out if it is used in your area. How does this approach meet the needs of children who have autism?

12 Design a 'sensory room' – no limit on money.

13 Find out what activities and sports are available in your area for people with special needs. Consider helping at a club or event as a volunteer.

5

Some People who Work with Children who have Special Educational Needs

The range of people who work with children who have special educational needs (SEN) is considerable.

- There are those who work with them daily, such as teachers, learning support assistants and nursery assistants.
- Those who may see them once a week, such as a speech therapist, physiotherapist, occupational therapist, specialist teacher or Portage home visitor.
- Those who may see them perhaps once a year, such as an educational psychologist or school doctor.
- Those who may only have intermittent contact such as an early years teacher, the school nurse and other medical staff. The parents of some pupils may also receive help and guidance from members of social services, such as a child disability team.

Teachers

Nowadays, all children are entitled to education appropriate to their needs. A child may receive education in any one of many situations, such as:

- at home
- mainstream school (nursery, primary, secondary)
- special school
- hospital.

In all of these places a child may receive attention from a teacher.

Teacher training and careers

There are two routes to obtaining a qualification as a teacher:

- Going to university to study for a Bachelor of Education degree (B.Ed).

This will be a four-year course combining theory and plenty of practical work in schools.

● Taking a Bachelor's degree in any subject. Then doing a supplementary course, usually one year full-time, to obtain a Post-graduate certificate in education (known as a PGCE course).

Students have to decide whether they wish to train to be a primary or secondary teacher. All teachers are now considered to be teachers of children with SEN.

Once qualified a teacher can apply for jobs in either the public or private sectors, anywhere in the country. After some years of experience a teacher may choose to take additional training in a specific area, such as teaching pupils with a visual impairment or those with severe learning difficulties.

One very important point in providing education for children who have SEN is early identification. The sooner a child's needs are identified, the sooner the appropriate support can be provided.

The early years worker plays an essential role in the early identification of a child's special needs. Here we can consider the work of early years workers.

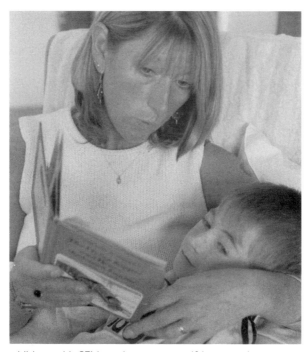

Teaching and helping children with SEN can be a very gratifying experience.

Early years workers

Some children have special needs from birth. Some show signs of having special needs in the early years before going to school. Others may or may not have special needs but are causing parents concern. Some early years workers are trained as teachers, and are sometimes called pre-school teachers; some have followed a child care course. Whatever the training, early years workers in nurseries often work with children who have SEN.

A pre-school teacher may be asked to visit the child in his home to make an assessment. Georgina is a pre-school teacher who works for a local education authority (LEA). She explained what happens.

'There are three pre-school teachers in our service and two nursery nurses. We visit parents in their homes if they are concerned about the development of their child. They usually contact us directly or through their GP or a health visitor.

'One of us will visit the family. We talk with the parents. Then we get to know the child through play and observation. We can make a number of visits if necessary.

'If the child goes to a playgroup or nursery then we may make a visit to see the child there and talk with the staff.'

After this period of assessment the pre-school teacher has discussions with other professionals and the parents. 'We may decide that the child's needs are not significantly different from those of other children. Should we decide that the child may have special needs then we can arrange for regular input from our staff or trained social services support workers.

'If it looks as if a child does have learning difficulties then the pre-school teacher will contact the educational psychologist to begin the statementing process.

'When the day comes for the child to start school then the pre-school teacher can support the parents in making their child's needs known to the school. What the pre-school teacher offers is a really super support service for parents and their children.'

Charlotte is an assistant in a small nursery school. After studying at the local college of FE she obtained an NNEB Diploma.

'I worked for a family for a while,' she said, 'but I really wanted to work either in a nursery or a special school. As a student I had spent some time in a special school and found it really interesting.'

'I have been here for just over a year. I really enjoy it. We do have two children with special needs. One is Amanda, who has Down's syndrome. The other is Robert who has cerebral palsy. They join in all the activities with the other children. There are no distinctions made.'

'I think it is really good that they are here with all the other children. Nobody seems to take any particular notice of them. They just blend in. They do not really get special attention.

'I am happy in this job and I will stay here for quite a while, I hope. Maybe one day I will go and work in a special school. But I am not in a hurry to change.'

Special educational needs co-ordinator (SENCo)

As we saw in Chapter 1, all teachers are now considered to be teachers of children with SEN. They have acquired some basic knowledge about meeting children's SEN. However, it would be impossible for them to have in-depth expertise across the whole range of SEN.

This is where advisor teachers have an important part to play. These are specialist teachers, for example for pupils with hearing impairment or visual impairment. They visit schools in their area, providing specialist input. (See Chapter 4 for further details.)

Whilst all teachers in schools should have a basic knowledge of SEN there is one teacher who has particular knowledge: the special educational needs co-ordinator. The 'Code of Practice ...' introduced the idea that all schools should have a special educational needs co-ordinator (known as SENCo).

The job of the co-ordinator is one of the most important in a school, especially a school where there is a large number of children with SEN. The co-ordinator is the person responsible for ensuring that the school's SEN policy is put into practice.

To give some idea of what this entails, we can meet a primary school SENCo.

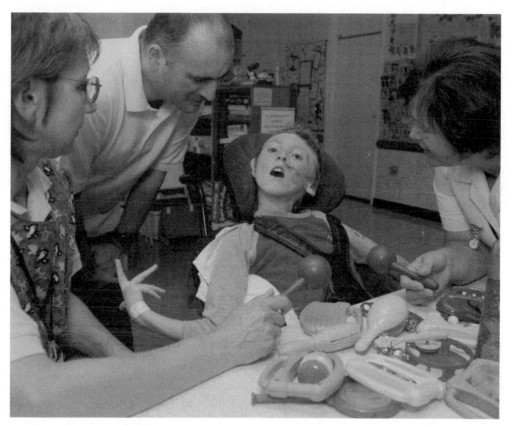

Cerebral palsy can cause difficulties in movement and speech

Sue is a SENCo. She teaches in a city primary school. Now in mid-career, she has many years of experience of working with children who have a wide range of SEN. Important as her role is in the school, she still teaches a class of ten-year-olds for four and a half days a week. She is also subject co-ordinator for science. As you can guess, she is one very busy person.

'We have 200 pupils in the school. About 50 of them have special needs,' Sue explained. 'Of that 50, fifteen have statements.'

'As SENCo my role is to overview the whole school. Part of my job is to look at the pupils who may have special needs and decide on priorities.'

Sue's experience over many years is of great significance. Newly qualified teachers do not have her depth of experience to draw on when they are considering whether or not a child has special needs.

'Young teachers tell me about a child who they feel may have some kind of learning difficulty,' Sue said. 'I spend some time in the class either working with the child or observing him.'

Sue then discusses the child with the class teacher. If they decide that the child does have special needs, then, together, they draw up an individual education plan (IEP).

As and when necessary Sue puts on staff training sessions. These are particularly important for staff who have recently joined the school. 'Our special needs policy depends very much on all staff understanding it and being involved in it,' she said.

An important part of Sue's work is liaising with the local authority SEN support teacher. This is a teacher who travels from school to school in the authority's area, giving support and guidance to staff. There are a number of such teachers in the area, for primary and secondary schools.

'The support teacher comes here once a week. We discuss children.

Together we work out a week's work for the pupil. Learning support assistants are very important in providing extra support for children.'

If it seems that a child may need assessment for a possible statement of SEN, Sue is a central figure in the process. She discusses a pupil with the educational psychologist and fixes an appointment. Sue organises the necessary investigations by various specialists. She also completes related paperwork.

Dealing with parents is another very important responsibility. 'I find that some parents of a child with special needs like to keep in contact with me as well as with the class teacher,' She said. 'I have known some of the parents for several years. Also, when a child is coming up to 11 and transferring to secondary school, it may be necessary to consider a special school placement. I usually take the parents to see the appropriate schools in the area.'

In Sue's school there are children with a wide range of special needs. They are all integrated into the school. Some, such as those with visual or hearing impairment, receive additional teaching or support from visiting specialist teachers.

As well as considering those children who have, or may have, learning difficulties, Sue also pays attention to the very able or gifted children. 'We do have a few children who are particularly able in one subject – maths, for example.' She has to ensure that their special needs are identified and met.

Learning support assistant

Children with SEN often need additional help from an adult. In school that help may be provided by a learning support assistant – usually referred to as an LSA. They are also known in some schools as Special Support Assistants – SSA.

The work of a learning support assistant

As the approach to educating children with SEN has changed over the years, so the demands of the LSA have changed. Broadly speaking, we can say that there has been a shift from an emphasis on care to an emphasis on education.

Teaching is often in small groups

Around 20 years ago people going into this work were often referred to as 'classroom assistant' or 'welfare assistant'. The work was fairly straightforward – helping children with dressing, toileting, feeding; helping to set out and clear away materials in the classroom; maybe some supervision of small groups of pupils during playtimes and some supervision in class.

Now, the work of an LSA is far more complex with important input into the teaching of children. As a member of the educational team, an LSA may be actively involved in a number of activities:

- academic work with children
- delivering therapy programmes under the direction of a specialist
- helping with independence training in dressing, feeding, toileting
- contributing to record-keeping
- planning work with the class teacher
- supporting integration of individual pupils.

In these and many other ways, the LSA makes a crucial contribution to the education and development of pupils.

Qualifications

There are no formal qualifications needed to become a LSA. However, it is true to say that an increasing number of people who apply for LSA posts do have qualifications. Some hold NNEB or BTEC qualifications; others have qualifications in nursing, social work or education. Then there are others who have qualifications and skills that may not appear to have direct relevance to the work.

More important than formal qualifications are personal qualities. The work of an LSA is demanding and varied. An LSA needs a range of skills and knowledge, patience, tolerance and initiative. It is important to be able to work as a committed member of a team. In some situations fitness is essential to cope with the physical demands of the job, such as lifting pupils.

Training and careers

Just as no formal qualifications are required, there is no obvious training for the job. Some LEAs organise training courses for people already in post. Individual schools may also offer in-service training and good quality induction programmes for new members of staff.

Whilst there will always be a need for LSAs in schools and colleges, there is no career structure. This is regrettable but one day it may change.

Kate is a LSA. She has a BTEC qualification in Childhood Studies. After leaving college she got a job in a special school. She has worked there for three years.

'I always knew that I wanted to work with children. As part of my BTEC course I went on a placement to a special school. It took me a little while to get used to it. By the time I left I knew that, if possible, I would like to get a job working with children who have special needs.

'This is my first job. I really enjoy it. At the moment I am an assistant in a primary class of six-to-eight-year-olds. There are eight children in the class. They all have severe learning difficulties. I have read up their notes. The causes of their difficulties vary.

'Every day is different. All the children have an individual education plan. Paula, the teacher, discusses things with me and I work with pupils either individually or in small groups. It might be computer work, or reading and writing activities or basic number work. I help the physiotherapist and carry out a programme for one little girl. I also help with riding once a week. We go to a stables a few miles away.

'As a class we have a swimming session once a week. We do music and movement with another class two mornings in the gym. Then we have a morning out in the school bus. We are doing a project on houses at the moment.

'Then, of course, I help with lunchtime, toileting, dressing and generally looking after the children. If one has an "accident" we may have to bath them.

'I really enjoy the work. As I say, it is very varied. I like the responsibility. It is satisfying to see even small changes and developments in children.

'We all work well as a team. That is another thing I like about the job. We all get on and help each other. And we have lots of laughs. It is tiring though. Physically and mentally. I am pretty worn out by the end of the day. But I would not want to do anything else. Not yet anyway. I am very happy here.'

Therapists

Special therapy may be needed for some children. This is often provided in school. The greatest need seems to be for speech and language therapy and physiotherapy. There are children who may benefit from occupational therapy, music therapy and aromatherapy. Occasionally, a play therapist may be involved in a child's education.

Speech and language therapist

Language is our tool for thinking. Speech is the usual way in which we communicate with each other using language. Some children have difficulties in using language. Some have difficulties in actually communicating through speech. Speech and language therapy is a way of helping these children to tackle their difficulties.

Speech therapy

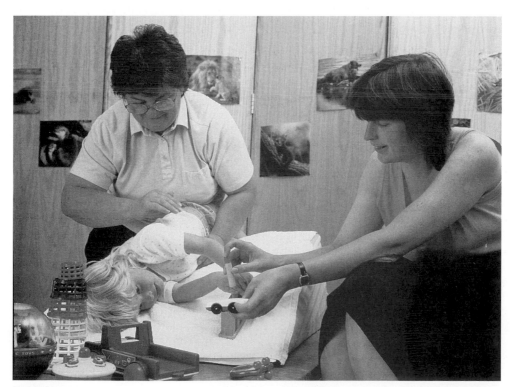

Physiotherapy

SPEECH AND LANGUAGE THERAPY

Until quite recently this therapy was known as 'speech therapy'. The emphasis was on helping children to improve the quality of their speech – articulation, clarity of pronunciation, and so on. Those who had severe difficulties were often taught other ways of communicating what they had to say through a signing system such as Makaton.

Gradually the work of the speech therapists has developed. Now, they are deeply involved with the actual language that children use. Some children have very little language – so what and how can they communicate? Other children may have plenty of language but do not know how to use it correctly. Yet others have language but are unwilling or unable to make use of it.

The former speech therapists are now working on actual language problems of children as much as the speech problems. Hence the change of job title.

In the course of their work therapists first assess children and diagnose the nature of the speech and language difficulties. Then, if therapy is considered appropriate, a programme is created specifically for the individual. Delivery of the programme over a period of weeks or months can involve the co-operation of many people, including school staff and parents.

THE CLIENTS

Children are the main client group for speech and language therapy. This may seem obvious enough. As young children are taking the first steps in learning language and speech skills, it is important to give them all the help possible if they are having problems. A child who has difficulty communicating with others can become a very frustrated person. And the frustration can lead to emotional and behavioural problems.

There is a need for similar work with some adults. Unfortunately, due to the shortage of therapists, many adults who need this form of therapy do not get it.

WHERE SPEECH AND LANGUAGE THERAPISTS WORK

Speech and language therapists work in a variety of settings. They work in hospitals, NHS clinics, special schools, mainstream schools and units. There is scope for private work which can be carried out in a client's home.

Training and Careers

A number of colleges and universities offer degree-level courses that can lead into the profession. There are also post-graduate courses available in some institutions. As mentioned, there is a shortage of qualified speech and language therapists. However, because of financial constraints many potential job opportunities are not available. This is a frustration for qualified therapists and a loss for possible clients. Those who are in employment often have heavy workloads. The career structure is limited to promotion to management positions.

Lesley is a qualified speech and language therapist. Since qualifying she has worked for over ten years. Most of her work has been in special schools and at a community clinic. She has done a small amount of work with adults in hospital.

'Most of my time is spent in special schools. Children are referred to me by teachers or the school doctor. Occasionally parent get in touch with the service about their child.

Children are referred for a range of reasons. A child may have unclear speech, or restricted speech. There may be problems with language. A child may only use very short sentences. There may be a problem of fluency in which the child stammers. Then there are more complex problems. For example, a child may have an all-round developmental age of, say, six years but language skills more appropriate to a three-year-old.

'My first job is to assess the child. I use standardised tests. I observe the child in different situations – in the classroom, at lunchtime, at playtime. Then I discuss the child with teachers and parents.'

'After the assessment a decision is made as to whether therapy is going to be appropriate. It is not always appropriate. It may be a matter of giving some guidance to parents and teachers.'

'In cases where therapy is considered appropriate it is always important to involve parents and teachers. They need to know what is happening so that they can support the therapy.'

'Sometimes therapists create the programme and it is delivered by teachers and learning support assistants in school. Children are either seen individually or in small groups. Where school staff carry out the programme the therapist has regular discussions with them to monitor progress and decide if any changes need to be made.

'There is quite a lot of paper work and administration. Records have to be written up. Reports have to be written for case conferences. Therapists often attend the Annual Reviews of children who have statements of SEN.'

'Speech and language therapy can be very beneficial for children. Unfortunately, the demand for the service far exceeds what we can offer.'

Physiotherapist

For most children physical movement comes naturally. From a very early age children explore their world through movement. A baby wriggles, crawls, learns to walk, climbs, jumps, and so on.

The basis for growth and learning is physical activity. Throughout life we are forever on the move. Recreational activities and sport are often based on movement. Without movement life is very restricted.

For some children, physical movement presents serious difficulties. There are many cause of the difficulties. For example, a child may be born with a particular condition that restricts movement. Another may have a disease in which physical skills deteriorate over time. Through injury another may only have limited movement skills.

This small minority of children need therapy to help them in the daily struggle against their physical disabilities. Physiotherapy provides that help.

PHYSIOTHERAPY

Physiotherapy is concerned with physical movement, the functioning of limbs, joints and muscles. It is a form of therapy that brings help to adults and children. The range of conditions treated with physiotherapy is extensive. It includes such things as injuries, outcomes of disease, congenital abnormalities and post-operative support.

As well as providing hands-on treatment, a physiotherapist will teach people how to avoid physical injury to their own muscles and joints. This preventative work is most important for children and adults. Staff who work with children who have physical disabilities often have to lift them. Lifting, if done incorrectly, can cause serious back injuries to staff.

The field of physiotherapy is wide. As a result therapists sometimes choose to specialise in one area. In schools you are most likely to meet a therapist who is a specialist in working with children.

PATIENTS

The range of children seen by the physiotherapist is considerable. Age-wise, they go from very young through to pupils in the secondary years. Referrals for physiotherapy come from a medical practitioner. Some children may need physiotherapy for a short period of time; others will need attention throughout their school career.

WHERE PHYSIOTHERAPISTS WORK

As far as children with SEN are concerned, most of the physiotherapy is delivered in schools. Some special schools, for example, will have a physiotherapy room with a therapist in attendance full-time. Units in mainstream schools may also have a permanent therapist. In other situations the physiotherapist may visit a number of pupils in different schools each week. They also visit children in their homes or work in child clinics based in hospitals and community clinics.

In the clinics physiotherapists sometimes run weekly groups for young children who have motor problems. These groups used to be known by such negative names as 'The Clumsy Group'. Now they are sometimes known as the 'Dyspraxic group' or something similar. Not many people will know what that means. At least it is not so obviously derogatory as 'clumsy'.

Physiotherapists are often employed by the local health authority. Some choose to go into private practice.

TRAINING AND CAREERS

Several colleges and universities offer degree courses. These last from three to four years. After graduation therapists can become state registered. This is essential for a therapist who wishes to work in a local health authority or the NHS.

In addition to qualified physiotherapists there are trained helpers who work under the direction of a physiotherapist.

Career opportunities are not great. As in other therapy work the career structure is limited. There are some openings for progression to a management position or into teaching.

Val is a physiotherapist, specialising in work with children. After some general work in a hospital she is now employed in a unit in a mainstream secondary school.

'The unit was set up some years ago,' she explained, 'to integrate children with special needs into a comprehensive school. We have 20 boys and girls here. As well as having learning difficulties, many of them also have physical difficulties.'

'The aim of our work is to try and help each child to reach his physical potential. Most of the children who come here have had physiotherapy when they were in primary school. I liaise with the physio working in the primary school.'

If a child has never had physiotherapy before coming into the unit and now appears to need some attention, the first thing Val does is carry out an assessment. She looks at such things as muscle tone, abilities in different positions, sitting and standing posture.

'If, after assessment, it is felt that physiotherapy would be beneficial then a programme of treatment is drawn up. Long-term and short-term aims are considered. I discuss the programme with the teacher and LSAs.'

The programme is then delivered by the physiotherapist and the LSAs – often on a daily basis.

Holidays can present a problem. It is obviously important that a programme of physiotherapy is provided all year round. To meet this need, Val will visit children at home during the holiday. She also teaches parents how to carry out the programme.

Val works closely with the occupational therapist who visits the school weekly. 'We discuss programmes together,' she explained.

She also has meetings with the speech and language therapist who comes to the school. 'It is very important that we all work together.'

As in all jobs there is paper work to keep up with. It is important to keep pupil records up to date. All the children in this particular unit have statements which are reviewed once a year. Val writes a report for that review and, where possible, attends the review meeting.

Occupational therapist

As we go about our daily lives we use all kinds of tools, machines, instruments and equipment. Most of the time we give little thought to all the skills that we need and use. From a very early age we are learning to use things. We learn to dress, to use toiletry articles, to cook and wash up, to play with all sorts of toys, to ride bicycles, to use domestic equipment, and so on.

Some people have serious difficulties with these activities. Their difficulty may arise from an accident or injury, from illness or from some congenital impairment. If they are to overcome their difficulties, then they need help. And they can get help from an occupational therapist.

OCCUPATIONAL THERAPY

Occupational therapy has grown and developed over the years. It is now a well-established form of therapy that helps adults and children to learn or re-learn skills necessary for daily life.

Children are our main concern here. Occupational therapy can help them to learn basic skills, introduce them to a range of play equipment and encourage them to explore the environment. Whilst learning new physical skills, the children will also be exercising their bodies and developing thinking skills.

There is a close link between occupational therapy and physiotherapy. The two therapies complement each other. In some schools you will find that the occupational therapist and the physiotherapist work closely together.

PATIENTS

You could say that anybody in need, child or adult, is a potential patient. Very young children with serious restrictions on physical activities are often given priority for therapy. They may have little self-motivation to learn skills and explore the world around them. Other children, with a range of limiting conditions, are also possible patients.

WHERE OCCUPATIONAL THERAPISTS WORK

Occupational therapists work in a range of settings. They hold sessions in hospitals and clinics, visit elderly people in residential homes, provide therapy in a person's home. They also work in schools – special schools in particular.

TRAINING AND CAREERS

There is a variety of ways of training to become an occupational therapist. There are training schools, often attached to hospitals, where you can study for a degree. Then there are post-graduate diploma courses. There are also training courses for people who wish to become a qualified support worker.

As in many of the therapies, career opportunities can be rather limited.

Muriel has been an occupational therapist for many years. She works in a large town. She is employed by the local health trust. Her experience has been very varied. Now she concentrates on working with children. She divides her week between a small number of schools.

'The aim of our work is to encourage independent living skills,' Muriel explained. 'I work in close liaison with the physiotherapists.'

In the schools allocated to her, Muriel is usually approached by a teacher who is anxious about some aspect of a pupil's physical skills. A child might have difficulty holding cutlery, for example. Or maybe a child shows a serious fear of being off the ground in the gym. In another instance, a child may not be sitting well in a chair.

As you can see, there is an overlap with the concerns of the physiotherapist. 'I will assess a child and then draw up a programme,' Muriel said. 'It is often important for the child to have therapy on a daily basis. So I work closely with the staff in a class and they deliver

> the programme as necessary. I come in once a week and we discuss progress.'
>
> As part of her week's work, Muriel also runs a group for children with dyspraxia. 'We hold the group at the child development centre at the hospital. It is for young children who have problems with motor skills. The parents bring the children and we work together as a group.'
>
> As with the physiotherapist, Muriel's work involves a number of children who have statements of SEN. She prepares written reports and usually attends the annual reviews.

Music therapist

Communication through speech is the way human beings usually make contact with each other. However, some children do not have speech. For a variety of reasons some children are unable to express themselves in language whether it be spoken, written or signed.

Music is a special way of communicating through which children can express and explore their feelings. They can also relate to each other, forming relationships through musical sounds. For children who are trapped in an invisible prison where communication with others seems to be impossible, music can be a way of escape.

MUSIC THERAPY

Music therapy is a means for children to communicate with others. The professional who delivers this form of therapy is a music therapist. In music therapist 'talk' the child is referred to as a client – not a pupil.

By using musical instruments and the voice to produce sounds, the music therapist and child can contact each other. They can form a relationship through the growth of a private musical language.

Music therapy is not to be confused with music lessons in the traditional sense. The child does not learn to play a musical instrument. In a sense, any objects that create musical sounds can be used for music therapy. It is not restricted to recognised musical instruments. In music therapy the music is usually improvised.

Communicating through music

THE CLIENTS

An ever-increasing range of children and adults are being introduced to music therapy as a way of expression and self-exploration. These include children and adults with physical, sensory, cognitive and emotional difficulties, those who have speech and language disabilities, people with mental illness and the elderly.

WHERE MUSIC THERAPISTS WORK

Music therapists work in a range of places including nurseries, schools, hospitals, community centres and prisons. A vast number of schools are understanding the value of music therapy for pupils with SEN. Special schools, in particular, are employing music therapists to work with those pupils for whom communication with others presents serious difficulties.

Therapists may be self-employed and work in private practice or employed by LEAs' hospital trusts and social services.

Training and Careers

It is usual for a music therapist to have a first degree in Music. After that, music therapy can be studied as a post-graduate subject, full-time or part-time. There are only a handful of colleges offering relevant courses at present. As the value of music therapy is becoming more widely known, so the demand for training courses is increasing. Career opportunities may well increase in coming years.

Shirley is a music therapist. After taking a degree in Music she taught in an infant school. There she became interested in children who had SEN. So she decided to combine this interest with her musical skills and knowledge. She went back to college full-time for one year to take a post-graduate qualification in Music Therapy. Now she works for a LEA.

'I work part-time in two special schools,' Shirley explained. 'In the schools I discuss pupils with the teachers. My priority is children who have no verbal communication skills. Once a pupil is selected for music therapy, sessions can go on over many years. I generally work with children from about three years of age up but there are mother and toddler groups which include younger children.'

'Usually a child will attend sessions once a week. Most of the work is done on a one-to-one basis. I also take small groups of pupils together – up to six in a group. Sessions last about half an hour, though in some instances a session may be no more than ten minutes. It all depends on the individual child.'

'We use a range of instruments. The piano and percussion instruments mainly – drums, gongs, bells, triangles, tambourines and so on.'

'Each pupil has their own programme with specific aims. Using the instruments we might aim to develop self-expression, listening skills or concentration. Over a period of time a constructive relationship can develop. The work also contributes to the development of self-esteem, confidence and interactive play skills.'

'For some pupils the music therapy session can provide a valuable change from the classroom. Here we can provide a more relaxed environment where the child has more time to respond. This is important for some children.

'Music therapy definitely works. It works as therapy and contributes to an individual pupil's general development. Whilst progress may be slow in some pupils with SEN, I find it very satisfying to see them making progress.'

Educational psychologist

The educational psychologist is a key person in the whole world of SEN. The EP (as they are sometimes known) may be involved in a wide range of activities including:

- assessing children, at the request of the school, to help define a child's particular learning difficulties
- contributing to the statementing process
- advising schools about ways of working with pupils who have learning difficulties or emotional and behavioural problems
- advising parents
- working with individual children.

Training and careers

The training extends over several years. The first requirement is a degree in psychology. Then you have to qualify as a teacher, usually by gaining a post-graduate certificate in education. After at least two years of teaching experience, a further year's full-time training is necessary to gain an MSc degree in educational psychology. That said, there are changes on the way, extending the training to doctoral level.

Where educational psychologists work

The majority of educational psychologists work for LEAs either full- or part-time. A few work for charities or private companies. A small number are self-employed. Most of their working hours are spent in schools.

Rachel is an educational psychologist. 'After taking my degree in psychology I trained as a teacher on a one-year PGCE course,' she said. 'I was happy to go into teaching and spent three years working in an inner city primary school. It was whilst I was teaching that I became increasingly interested in children who had learning difficulties.'

Rachel then decided that she would like to develop her career in a slightly different direction. 'I decided to explore the possibility of becoming an educational psychologist. I found a one-year MSc course and did a full-time course.'

Once qualified, she soon found a job with a LEA. 'I have been working as an educational psychologist with the same authority for six years now. I like the job; it is varied. I have responsibility for a number of schools scattered over quite a wide area. The schools include a comprehensive, several primary schools and two special schools.'

Rachel works with a great age range of children from pre-schoolers through to 19-year-olds. 'Children are referred to me by a paediatrician. At present the youngest child I am seeing is a boy of three months. He has Down's syndrome. I have been to his home a few times. My main purpose is to get to know him, to discuss matters with his parents, identify their concerns and let them know what services are available. I also liaise with early years workers.'

In due course this little boy will need a statement of SEN. Rachel sets the statementing process in motion. That means more formal contact. 'I use developmental checklists and carry out a number of tests combined with observations. The aim is to get as full a picture as possible of his development in all areas, such as speech, play, social skills.'

After a statement of SEN has been agreed by all parties, Rachel continues her involvement with the child. 'Educational psychologists are invited to the child's annual review. Depending on the nature of the child's needs, I might visit him in school during the year.'

Rachel keeps in close contact with the teachers in her range of schools. In particular, she is familiar with those children who are on the SEN

Register. 'I spend a lot of time with teachers,' she explained. 'We may discuss pupils in general. Often there are specific concerns that teachers want to go over. For example, a child may have emotional difficulties or his behaviour may be causing concern. We can work together and agree on a behaviour plan. We share this with the parents too.'

Whilst most of her time is spent in schools, meeting pupils, their parents and staff, Rachel also has to maintain links with education officers and social services personnel. Then there are reports to be written and case conferences to attend. Being an educational psychologist is a busy life – but one that Rachel enjoys.

Volunteer

Finally in this section I should like to mention volunteers. In nurseries, playgroups, primary schools, secondary schools and special schools you will find people giving their time to help in the classroom. Sometimes they are parents of children in the school. But not always.

Being an unpaid volunteer in a school is a good way of experiencing a job without taking on a heavy commitment. Over the years I have known many people who have approached schools asking if they can work as a volunteer. Often they have been young men and women, keen to explore a possible career.

There are two valuable aspects of working as a volunteer:

- you can try out the job
- the employer can see you in action.

It is not uncommon for a volunteer to move on to a paid position, should a vacancy arise in the school. Failing that, some volunteers are in an excellent position to apply for a vacancy in another school.

Of course, not all volunteers are exploring a possible career. Many are very happy being a part of the educational team on a voluntary basis, full-stop. They can make a very valuable contribution to education, especially the education of children who have SEN.

Swimming is an enjoyable form of therapy

ACTIVITIES and QUESTIONS

1   Think back to your own school days. Did any specialist staff visit the school to work with pupils who had SEN? Discuss with other students.

2   Choose one special needs related profession that interests you in particular. Find out as much as you can about it. Write up your findings.

3   See if you can 'shadow' a therapist in a school for a day and invite someone in to talk to a group of you. Discuss the experience with other students.

4   Learning support assistants play a very important role in the education of children with SEN. Find out just what an LSA does in a school of your choice.

5   If you visit a school, try to have a discussion with the SENCo. What are the main responsibilities of the job?

6

Issues to Consider

In this chapter we will look at a handful of issues related to children who have special educational needs (SEN). These are important matters. In some instances people have different opinions about the issues. They are presented here as aspects of special needs that you may like to think about and discuss.

The issues we are going to look at are:

Models of disability

There are different ways of considering people who have disabilities. The way you consider them, the framework that you use, is your 'model of disability'. It is extremely important for it influences all your interactions, choices and decisions. (See page 119.)

We shall look at two models: the Medical Model and the Social Model.

OFSTED Inspection

Inspection of schools and colleges by Ofsted inspectors has brought many changes in the education of children with SEN. Not everybody considers the changes appropriate. (See page 119.)

Inclusion

The inclusion of children with SEN in mainstream schools is now a legal requirement – with a few exceptions. There may be difficulties for some schools. However, schools must show real commitment to providing resources to enable all children to access the curriculum and share in the school community. (See page 116.)

Equal opportunities

In all sorts of ways people with special needs have been the victims of discrimination. It has not always been intentional. It is important that we all look at ourselves to see if we are guilty of denying equal opportunities to people with special needs. (See page 122.)

Advocacy

This links with equal opportunities. Some people who have special needs are unable to speak up for themselves. Their views and wishes may never be known. There is a growing move to change this. Advocacy is the activity in which somebody puts forward the views and wishes of another person. This can lead to self-advocacy for some. (See page 124.)

Very Able children

It may seem odd to include very able children in this book. They may not have learning difficulties. However, many of them do have special needs. And all too often those needs are neglected. Again, there is a growing movement for change to ensure that their needs are identified and met. (See page 127.)

Post-19 provision

Here, again, you may think that this issue is a little out of place in this book. However, it is such an important issue that it is included. Children's needs are now identified and, with varying degrees of success, met in schools. On leaving school a small minority of children discover that provision no longer exists. What can they do? What can their parents do? (See page 129.)

Training/teacher education

The success or failure of the education of children with SEN depends to a large extent on the quality of training offered to the people who work with them: teachers, early years workers, learning support assistants (LSAs). As far as teachers in particular are concerned, there is some fear that the present system of teacher education does not prepare all teachers adequately. (See page 131.)

Special schools – do they have a future?

There are people who argue for segregated provision. People who believe that the needs of some children are best met in a special school, segregated from the mainstream. Remember, what makes a special school special is that it offers special provision for children with SEN. And that is one of the strong arguments put forward to keep special schools, at least for some children.

There are a number of types of special school. Usually they are small schools that cater for a specific range or type of SEN. For example, there are schools for children with SLD, schools for children with autism, schools for children with hearing impairments.

As an example, we can consider a school for children who have SLD. Here we will summarise the main features of such a school.

The school caters for 60 pupils, from 2 to 19 years of age. The teachers have a variety of specialist qualifications relevant to the needs of the pupils. The LSAs also have relevant qualifications or experience. The staff includes a number of therapists. Children are taught in small classes or groups with no more than 12 pupils per class. There is a hydrotherapy pool, a sensory room and a number of other special resources. Children follow the National Curriculum according to the level of their ability.

SOME GAINS OF SPECIAL SCHOOL PROVISION FOR PUPILS WITH SEN

- Staff with special skills and expertise
- a range of therapists and specialist services
- small classes or teaching groups that make the delivery of individual educational programmes more manageable
- resources appropriate for the needs of the pupils
- opportunities for friendships with other pupils with SEN
- a protective environment
- a secure base from which to explore the world around.

These are some of the gains. You may be able to think of more. (See page 118.)

Inclusion

The early years of the 21st Century should be good for children who have special educational needs. They should benefit from a growing national- and international-commitment to inclusion in schools and society in general.

Let's go over once again what we mean by inclusion – and why it is so important. Inclusion is a process. It means including children who have

SEN in mainstream schools. It is their right to go to the same school as their brothers, sisters and friends.

There are two conditions. One, their parents want them to go to a mainstream school rather than a special school. Two, they will not detract from the education of other children.

The developing legal support for inclusion

The legal requirement for the inclusion of children with SEN in mainstream schools has been a long time coming. Remember how before 1970 some children were considered ineducable. That seems extraordinary today. Then we had the drive for integration – a useful step towards inclusion. And now, inclusion is with us.

You could say that the 1990s was the decade that ushered in inclusion as an international process. The Education Act 1993 introduced inclusion, as a legal requirement, to the UK. Not very much happened in schools.

In 1994 UNESCO announced its commitment to inclusion on an international scale. The Salamanca Statement (so-called because the world conference was held in Salamanca, Spain) urged all governments to pursue the principle of inclusive education.

1997 saw a further commitment in the UK when the government published the Green Paper, 'Excellence for All Children – Meeting Special Educational Needs'. This confirmed that inclusion was to be promoted in schools.

The full legal support for inclusion came in the SEN and Disability Act 2001. All maintained schools must be prepared to accept children with SEN.

Practical matters

Of course, what is written in official documents may not transfer 100% to schools. There will always be discussion about the inclusion of all children in mainstream schools.

There are parents of children with SEN who do not want their child to go to a large, bustling, mainstream school. They argue that the needs of their child are best met in a small special school where there are specialist staff and special resources.

There are some teachers and other staff in mainstream schools who recognise that, at present, they do not have the knowledge or skills necessary to work effectively with some children with SEN.

Schools may not have the resources to adapt their buildings and facilities so that any child with SEN can access the school and the curriculum as an equal of other children.

However, inclusion is here to stay. It is a process that will see change in schools over the next few years. There may well be difficulties for individual schools. There may be some reluctance to make expensive provision.

The bottom line is that it is the right of any child to attend a mainstream school – as long as the two conditions are fulfilled (parents' wishes, the education of other children is not hindered).

The role of special schools

So what about special schools? Do they still have a place?

Ever since the idea of integration was defined in the early 1980s there has been debate about special schools. If there are serious educational benefits to be gained from integrating children with SEN on a part-time basis what is the need for special schools? What do they offer that mainstream doesn't? What are their disadvantages? If local authorities can provide qualified, experienced staff with appropriate resources in a mainstream setting – who needs special schools?

The debate engages strong feelings both for and against. The truth is that with the legal support of the SEN and Disability Act 2001 there is a guaranteed place for special schools in some form or other. The Act acknowledges that probably there will always be a few children who will not be able to cope with a mainstream setting. They will go to a special school.

There may be another role for special schools. Staff may be asked to help develop the knowledge and skills of mainstream colleagues so that they can provide appropriate education for the influx of children with SEN.

It is likely, of course, that some special schools will close in the next few years. As the inclusion of more children with SEN into mainstream schools becomes a reality so there will be less need of so many special schools.

Conclusion

Inclusion is a process. In the coming years there will be far more children with SEN in mainstream schools. This shift has international support and national legislation to back it up. There will always be a place for some special schools.

Inspection

The Office for Standards in Education is better known as OFSTED. Trained Ofsted inspectors spend time in all schools. Their aim is to identify good points and weaknesses in a school as measured against certain criteria. They publish a report on the school which is available for anybody to read. It is worth reading the Ofsted report on a school if you are considering a job there.

Schools that have serious weaknesses – according to the Ofsted criteria – may be said to need 'special measures' to bring them up to standard. A greater percentage of special schools have need of 'special measures' than mainstream schools. Why do you think that is?

There are people working in special schools who consider that the Ofsted criteria for a successful school do not tie in with the needs of some children with SEN. What is the priority for a child who has profound and multiple learning difficulties? Certainly not being forced into a pre-set mould that was designed for mainstream children who do not have SEN.

There are staff and parents who disagree strongly with the Ofsted criteria. Especially as there are Ofsted inspectors who have limited or zero experience of teaching children with SEN. Scandalous? Some people think so.

It's all to do with the National Curriculum. Of course, a school can opt out of the National Curriculum. However, if a school does that there is another problem. If a school does opt out then children in the school are marginalised. They are put into the backwater of Education. That is not a nice thought.

So what is the way forward? You might like to discuss that.

Conclusion

Inspection has focused the minds of many people who work with children who have SEN. Standards in special schools have been raised – according to

Ofsted criteria. Not everybody considers Ofsted criteria and priorities to be appropriate for some children with SEN.

Models of disability

If you are not totally clear about models of disability, don't worry. You may not be able to explain the different models but you will certainly be using one or another. Let me try to clarify things.

You can think of a model as a way of considering a person. It's a way of putting an individual into some sort of framework that makes sense to you. Once you've put a person into a framework or a structure you then know how to deal with the person.

We will consider two major models:

- the Medical Model
- the Social Model.

There are other models but these two are the best known.

The Medical Model

In the Medical Model the focus is on the child – and his condition.

A child has a visual impairment. It is serious. He cannot see at all well. He has a **condition**. Once you understand his condition – visual impairment – you can provide **treatment**. You can do something to the child to help him see better. That is the core of the medical model. Two key words:

- condition
- treatment.

The focus of treatment is to make some positive change to the child. The child with a visual impairment might undergo surgery on his eyes to improve his vision. A child with a hearing impairment might be supplied with a hearing aid. A child who cannot walk might be given calipers or put in a wheelchair.

The Medical Model is a very helpful way of considering some children. However, it can have undesirable aspects as well.

If a person has a condition, in the medical sense, then by implication he is not normal. He differs from most people as a result of his condition. He is abnormal. You will remember how for many years before the Warnock Report (1978) some children with learning difficulties were officially referred to as being 'educationally subnormal' (ESN). Imagine what that does for a person's self-esteem. Also, such categorisation has a significant effect on the way other people relate to the so-called 'educationally subnormal' child.

The limitations of the Medical Model led to the development of another way of considering people with disabilities: the Social Model.

The Social Model

In the Social Model the focus of attention is on the environment in which the child lives.

Let's consider the child with a visual impairment. His visual impairment is part of his identity. He has every right to live a full life just as he is. So to facilitate his participation in society changes are made to the environment – the physical environment and the human environment.

Crossing busy roads at a pelican crossing can be hazardous for the child with a visual impairment. Have you noticed changes in the environment to help the child? At the crossing, red slabs with raised 'dots' to feel with the feet. And what about sounds? Pips to indicate when it is safe to cross.

In this example we can see how society says we will accept the person as he is. We will make changes so that he can participate on his own terms. There is no suggestion of abnormality; no negative impact on the person's self-esteem.

So which model do you consider best? Does it depend on the situation? Which model best enhances the self-respect of the person with a disability? Can you see which model you use with regard to children with SEN? There is often serious debate over the models and their effects.

As in so many things, each model has a valuable contribution to make. The child who cannot walk may be given a wheelchair – based on the Medical Model. Changes in the school environment might be made – ramps put in place, wider corridors built in new schools so that wheelchairs can move about easily. Such changes are based on the Social Model.

You can see that the Social Model underlies the philosophy of Inclusion.

Conclusion

There are two major models of disability: the Medical Model and the Social Model. The Medical Model focuses on making changes to the person. The Social Model focuses on making changes to the environment (including human attitudes). Each model has its uses. It is important to be aware of how a particular model conditions the way you interact with a person who has SEN. The Social Model underpins Inclusion.

Equal opportunities

Equal opportunities is a big subject. The first thought that comes to mind when you mention equality of opportunity is probably ethnicity – or maybe gender. After that you may think of age, marital status or disability. We are focusing our attention on disability.

What is equality of opportunity?

Sometimes you hear people say, 'All people are equal.' But are they? And in what sense? If you look at a group of boys and girls it is much easier to see the ways in which they are different. One is tall, another is small; one is ten years old, another is nine; one is good at swimming, another does really well in maths. You can spend a lot of time spotting differences.

We are not equal. We are all different from each other. You are different from your best friend in all sorts of ways. However, when it comes to various opportunities in life our differences can be taken into account. If your best friend is a wheelchair user and wants to go to the cinema with you, then access for a wheelchair is essential. If your friend and you are to have an equal opportunity of going to the cinema, then the cinema owner must acknowledge your friend's need and take steps to meet that need.

The same approach applies in a school. A girl who has a visual impairment will need certain resources so that she can have an equal opportunity with other pupils of having full access to the curriculum.

Language

The language we use provides a clue to our attitude to people. Three words we looked at in the Introduction are very important. Here they are again:

- impairment
- disability
- handicap
- an impairment refers to any physical or psychological loss or abnormality of development
- disability is the restriction of an activity caused by the impairment
- handicap is the personal disadvantage that a person experiences.

Language is very important in any discussions about equality of opportunity. We may not be able to do anything about a person's impairment. We may be able to do something to address the disability that arises from the impairment. We can do many things to ensure that the person's handicaps are reduced. By reducing handicaps we open the door to equality of opportunity.

How we describe people

One of the most important ways of ensuring equality of opportunity lies in the language we use. Often, offensive phrases or words trip off the tongue when people refer to those who have disabilities. Offensive words reveal an attitude. There is a world of difference between saying of a boy, 'He's a spastic' and saying, 'He has cerebral palsy.' Or again, between saying, 'She's a mongol' and, 'She has Down's syndrome.' It is most important to get words right. The right words will lead to the right attitude. And that will lead to respect, acceptance and the development of equal opportunities.

Avoiding stereotypes

Using offensive words or focusing on a person's disability easily lead us into the trap of stereotypes, assuming one specific quality in a group of individuals. So you hear people say, 'All Down's children are very loving.' Or 'Autistic children are talented.' The stereotypes deny individuality.

The simple key to getting things right when describing another person is to focus your attention on the person – as a person. Not the impairment. Not the disability. Not the handicap. We have referred to this in the Introduction. Indeed, it is one of the main themes of this book.

So, for example, David is David. David has an impairment. David may have a disability as a result of his impairment. As a result David may have a handicap. David is David. If we focus on the person, David, we will see that he has exactly the same rights as everybody else. He should have the same opportunities.

Equal opportunities in school

It should by now be clear that a child who has any kind of impairment should be given equal opportunities in education along with peers who do not have impairments. This does raise some interesting issues.

If all children are to have an equal opportunity for education and for accessing the curriculum, then schools must do everything possible to identify and meet each child's needs. Mainstream schools must provide all the resources needed to ensure equality of opportunity for all pupils.

What about segregated provision in a special school? Whilst the special school may have all the specialist resources that will meet the needs of the pupils, it could be argued that segregation is itself never going to offer equality of opportunity. Pupils who attend the special school will not have access to the rich variety of mainstream school. But the special school may be able to offer an equal opportunity to learn.

Our values and attitudes

Our attitudes grow from our values. If we value children as individuals then our attitude will be to aim to provide each individual with equal opportunities. No child will be 'better' than any other. No child will have preferred access to education. All children will have the same rights – and one of the main rights is to have equality of opportunity.

Conclusion

We have seen that children are all different. They are not equal. But they do have the right to equal opportunities in education. The language we use is most significant in creating a society in which equal opportunities flourish. Stereotypes prevent us from seeing children as individuals. We must work to see the individual. And we must work to identify and meet the needs of individuals. Segregated provision runs the risks of denying equality of opportunity. Finally, our attitudes grow from our values. If we value individuals then we will develop positive attitudes and encourage equality of opportunities for all individuals.

Advocacy

Put simply, advocacy means speaking on behalf of somebody else. Some people may have difficulties in expressing their own views, feelings and ideas. Children and young people with SEN may have considerable difficulty. Their case, in any situation, can be put by somebody else.

The person who talks on behalf of another person is an advocate.

Legal matters

In recent years the rights of the child have been emphasised. The Children Act 1989 make it clear that the views of the child are important. They must be heard and taken into account in any legal dispute about the child's welfare. The United Nations Convention on the Rights of the Child (1989) conveys a similar message. The Code of Practice 1994 states that the views of the child should be heard in matters concerning their education.

Rights in schools

In schools, children are not often involved in discussions and decision-making about the very things that affect their lives. Rarely are children, either primary or secondary, invited to give their opinions about such things as the time schools starts, the way the day is structured, rules about behaviour, and so on. These decisions are usually made by adults. Yet it is the children whose live are affected.

Prompted by legislation on the rights of children there is a gentle change going on. Some schools are involving children in discussions about such matters. With regard to pupils who have SEN, the lack of involvement in the decision-making has been even more obvious. They have rarely had a say in how school runs.

Why advocacy is important for people with SEN

Advocacy is important for all children. For young people who have SEN it is essential if their views are to be known. They are often very dependent on other people for all manner of things. Decisions are often made for them, without consultation. And yet they do have views on what they want for themselves. They may have difficulty in expressing their views. That is no reason to ignore them, assume that they do not have views, or treat them as being unimportant.

metimes children and young people with SEN have low self-esteem. mparing themselves with other children, they may feel inferior in one way or another. As a result, they do not think well of themselves. They may then believe that their opinions and ideas are inferior too. If nobody bothers to find out what they want, like or aspire to, then they may believe that other people also consider their viewpoint is not important. The downward spiral continues.

Equal opportunities, as we have seen, is an important issue. People with SEN do have the right to enjoy equal opportunities. They may need an advocate to stand up for these rights, to present their case. If nobody presents their case, then it is all too easy for society to ignore it.

Self-advocacy

In self-advocacy a person presents their own views. For many children with SEN this is a distinct possibility. In schools there is growing encouragement given to pupils to speak up for themselves. For example, children with SEN are invited to attend the annual review of their statement of special educational needs. However, there is much that remains to be done to create occasions for self-advocacy.

Conclusion

Advocacy is an important development. In recent years, with the strong support of legislation, the views of children are being heard and treated seriously. This process is extending to children with SEN. It may be a slow development. Some adults may feel threatened by it. But it is a process that should, and probably will, continue to expand into all areas of life.

Through advocacy, or self-advocacy, children with SEN are empowered. Their existence is valued. Their opinions are heard. Their dependence on adults can be reduced. Their independence can be increased.

Very able children

It may seem rather strange to include discussion of very able children in a book that focuses on children who have learning difficulties. These children may not have learning difficulties. But some of them do have SEN.

There is an increasing interest in education circles in the needs of very able children. The schools inspectorate (OFSTED) has highlighted the fact that often the most able pupils in a school are not receiving satisfactory education. Their special needs are not being met. Sometimes such pupils become bored with school and resort to disruptive behaviour.

Descriptive terms are always changing. 'Very able children' refers to those who are 'gifted' and those who are 'talented'.

'Gifted' refers to the child who has a high level of ability in many subjects and activities. He may or may not be achieving his potential.

'Talented' refers to the child who has a high level of ability in one subject – for example, singing or languages.

Identification of very able children

As mentioned, schools are becoming increasingly aware of this small group of children whose abilities are outstanding for their age. There are tests available to help in their early identification.

Once identified, what can schools do to meet the needs of these children?

There are three possible responses:

- segregation
- acceleration
- enrichment.

Segregation means putting all the very able children together. Acceleration moves the child up a year. Enrichment keeps the child with his peers with a special programme.

You will be able to see points for and against each approach.

The most usual approach is enrichment. This means differentiation.

Differentiation

Differentiation is the approach generally followed in addressing the SEN of pupils. This approach starts with the fact that each child is an individual and therefore different from other children. In an ideal world, every child would follow a curriculum tailored to his needs. The level of learning would be fine-tuned to build on the firm foundations of previous learning and provide attainable challenges in the present. Step-by-step success would be a real possibility. Such refinement of mass education must remain a dream.

Whilst differentiation is now the usual way that schools set about meeting the needs of children with learning difficulties, it is also the favoured approach to meeting the needs of very able children. Once identified as having outstanding ability, a pupil can then be given more individualised education.

Of course, from the point of view of the school, providing resources to meet a very able pupil's needs may become a problem. The school may not have the funds to pay for the additional resources. If the school decides to allocate funds to one particular pupil then, obviously, other pupils are deprived of resources. Whatever decision the school makes, you could argue that the needs of some pupils will not be met.

The answer is to look for assessment by the local authority so that a statement of SEN can be drawn up.

Conclusion

There is a small minority of pupils who have outstanding abilities in a range of activities both academic and recreational. These pupils my be described as very able. As such they may have SEN. Those needs may or may not be met by the school.

The first thing the school has to do is identify any children who are very able. Once identified, their needs can be addressed. It may be that the school can meet their needs. However, in some instances the resources cannot be provided from the school's budget. The answer, then, is to encourage the local authority to prepare a statement of SEN. With that, it should be possible for the school to have additional resources to meet the needs of the pupil.

Post-19 provision

At the age of 19 pupils leave secondary schooling. For most people the next step will be employment, or at least the search for employment, or further full-time study in an institution of further or higher education. For a small minority of people with SEN there is no obvious way ahead.

Perhaps we can look at this problem by focusing on one young man. Robert is 10. He has profound and multiple learning difficulties (PMLD). He lives with his parents, in a small house in a city suburb. He has one older brother who is a university student.

'We do not know what is going to happen to Robert,' says his mother. 'Our main worry is that we are getting older and do not see how we can look after him full-time at home.

'We love him dearly. We would like him to stay with us but we know that it is unrealistic. At the same time we do not really want him to go away. Not that there are many places for him to go. There are one or two community homes. Getting into them is difficult. There do not seem to be enough places.

'We do not see what we can do with him at home every day. My husband

goes to work and I have a part-time job. I would have to give up that. Robert went to a special school a few miles away. He was happy there. There was plenty going on and he took part in all sorts of activities – swimming, riding, music. He even went away with his class for a week at a holiday centre. If he stays here at home his life will be very limited. He is very heavy now. We cannot cope with him physically.

'There is a sort of day centre not far away. We have discussed the possibility of Robert going there. They might be able to take him one or two days a week. That is not certain. Plenty of people do want to help. Social services support us. But there just aren't the facilities. It seems that there are more people with special needs than there is suitable provision for them as adults.

'We have discussed the problem with other parents. Many seem to be in the same position. There just aren't the places for our children to go when they leave school. It is a terrible worry.'

Conclusion

Provision for school-leavers is patchy. It varies from region to region. The general feeling seems to be that the provision is not adequate to meet demand. Many parents are working hard to persuade local authorities and government to focus attention and resources on what will be a growing problem.

Training/teacher education

One of the points made in the Warnock Report 1978 was that all teachers should consider themselves to be teachers of pupils with SEN. That idea followed naturally from the Report's emphasis on integration. If pupils with SEN were to be educated in mainstream schools then any teacher might at any time have to teach one or more pupils with SEN.

This being so, all teachers would need some preparation for teaching pupils with SEN. The obvious time and place for this preparation was on initial teacher education (ITE) courses. So far so good. But what of teachers who were already working in schools who had had no preparation? Again, a fairly obvious answer. They should have opportunities to attend courses as part of their on-going professional development. Such courses are often referred to as INSET (In-Service Education and Training).

The set-up seemed to be fine – on paper. In reality, it did not work out quite as well as planned. For one thing, before these ideas were introduced, some teachers chose to specialise in a particular area of SEN. So, for example, if somebody wished to focus their career on teaching children with SLD they could go on a teacher education course with that special emphasis.

If all teachers were to be seen as teachers of children with SEN, then this kind of specialisation was not acceptable. As a result many courses, with a specific focus on SEN, closed down. A lot of expertise and accumulated experience was probably lost for ever.

Furthermore, colleges and universities that provided ITE now had to take on an added responsibility. Often they had neither the time nor the expertise to develop satisfactory courses.

The result of this was that whilst all teachers were asked to consider themselves as teachers of pupils with SEN, many did not have adequate preparation for this teaching. Newly qualified teachers (NQTs) could find that they had several pupils with statements in a class. How to meet their special needs was a serious problem.

What about in-service courses? Well, things were not so bad here. Some universities have put on courses on relevant SEN subjects for teachers. These might be full-time for one year or, more often, part-time over two years or more. Some LEAs also offered short courses for teachers. Overall, however, the numbers of teachers obtaining recognised specialist qualifications appears to have declined over the past 20 years.

The truth is that the situation since the Warnock Report and the Education Act 1981 has been far from satisfactory. Clearly something had to be done. In February 1996 a group known as the Special Educational Needs Training Consortium (SENTC) published their Report, *Professional Development to Meet Special Educational Needs*.

The Report starts from the position that all is not well. It then puts forward many detailed proposals about the knowledge and skills that teachers need if they are to teach pupils who have SEN. It is, if you like, a blueprint for future developments in teacher training with regard to SEN.

This is not really the place to go into the details of the Report. Should you be interested in knowing what range of skills and knowledge you might need in order to teach pupils with SEN, the Report is the ideal place to find the information. The Appendix lists the competencies required for all specialisms, for example, 'competencies required by teachers of pupils with autism', 'competencies required by teachers of pupils with multi-sensory impairment', and so on.

Conclusion

The majority of children with SEN are educated in mainstream schools. Any teacher will be expected to teach such pupils. All teachers need training in ways of identifying, assessing and meeting a child's special needs.

ACTIVITIES and QUESTIONS

1 Discuss the arguments for and against inclusion with other students.
2 What particular advantages are claimed for special schools?
3 Find out the policy on the inclusion of children with SEN in your area.
4 Discuss with a friend the meaning of the following words: impairment, disability, handicap.
5 With friends, brainstorm on words used about people who have special needs. Discuss the implications of these words.
6 Consider whether you hold in your mind any stereotypes about people with special needs. Share your discoveries with other students.
7 In what ways has Ofsted inspection of special schools had a positive effect? And negative?
8 What is advocacy
9 In what ways can you make your views known to the college authorities?
10 Why is advocacy an important issue for children with SEN?
11 In what ways does a very able child have special needs?
12 Explain 'differentiation'.
13 What is the policy of your LEA on very able children?
14 What provision is made in your area for school-leavers who have SEN?
15 If you are going to be a teacher, think about the knowledge and skills you might need so that you can be effective in working with children who have SEN. Discuss your ideas with other students.

Conclusion

The education of children who have special educational needs (SEN) has come a long way since 1970. Before the Education Act 1970 children who were described as 'mentally handicapped' were denied education. Now, all children have access to education.

Since 1970 there has been a steady movement to have all children educated together. Today, the great majority of children with SEN are educated with their peers in mainstream schools. This is a movement that is welcomed by most people. There may still be arguments in favour of segregated provision for a very small number of children. How long such provision will continue to exist is an interesting question.

There will always be some children who have SEN. They are entitled to the same quality of provision, the same opportunities as all other children. The quality of their education depends very much on the knowledge and skills of the people who work with them. Colleges and universities have the responsibility of ensuring that training courses for future professionals are of the very highest quality.

Appendix 1
Further Reading

There are hundreds of books and magazines in print about special educational needs (SEN). Nowadays most college libraries will have some of them on their shelves. Many public libraries have increased their stock of books on special needs in recent years.

This section contains some ideas for further reading. With a few exceptions, only books published since The Education Reform Act 1988 have been chosen. Things change so quickly that the information in books can soon be out of date. Beware of this when reading older texts. The titles are grouped according to each section of the book, though many could easily be put into different sections. The brief comments on each title may help you decide if the book is for you.

General

CAF Directory of Specific Conditions and Rare Syndromes (1991). (Third ed. 1995) London: Contact a Family. This is a most valuable reference book. It is in effect an encyclopaedia. There are hundreds of entries. The book comes as a ring binder with loose-leaf A5 format and is updated regularly. For each entry there is information about support groups, associations and services. Highly recommended.

Darnborough, A. & Kinrade, D. (compilers). (Eighth ed. 1999) *Directory for Disabled People*. Hemel Hempstead: Prentice Hall Europe. Useful reference book.

Farrell, M. (1997) (Second ed. 2000) *The Special Education Handbook*. London: Fulton. An A–Z reference book.

Lea, K. (1952) (Fourteenth ed. 1977) *Careers Encyclopedia*. London: Cassell. Information about many careers including some relevant to working with children who have SEN. Well worth consulting if you want some preliminary information about a possible career and qualifications needed.

Worthington, A. (ed.) (1999) *The Fulton Special Education Digest*. London: Fulton. A mine of information, addresses and websites.

Chapter 1

Brayne, H. & Martin, G. (1990) (Third ed. 1993) *Law for Social Workers*. London: Blackstone. There is a helpful breakdown and discussion of the Children Act. Child protection issues are examined.

Chastry, H. & Friel, J. (1991) *Children with Special Needs*. London: Kingsley. Assessment and the legal rights of parents.

DES (1978) *Special Educational Needs* (Warnock Report). London: HMSO. This Report has had a major impact on the education of children with SEN. Even though published in 1978, it is still well worth looking at.

DEF (1994) *Code of Practice on the Identification and Assessment of Special Educational Needs*. London: HMSO. An official document that explains in detail what schools are expected to be doing.

DFES (2002) (Revised Version). *SEN Code of Practice*, London: HMSO.

Harris, N. (1997) *Special Educational Needs and Access to Justice*. Bristol: Jordan. SEN tribunals is the subject. A book packed with facts, assessing how successful or not the system has been.

Jones, N. & Docking, J. (1992) *Special Educational Needs and the Education Reform Act*. Stoke-on-Trent: Trentham. Discusses issues that arise from the Act and their implications for the curriculum.

Solity, J. & Raybould, E. (1988) *A Teacher's Guide to Special Needs*. Milton Keynes: Open University. Detailed study of the Education Act 1981 and the implications for schools.

Whitney, B. (1993) *The Children Act and Schools*. London: Kogan Page. This is a helpful guidebook intended for teachers. It highlights the major parts of the act that are particularly relevant to schools. Worth looking at.

Chapter 2

Cornwall, J. (1996) *Choice, Opportunity and Learning*. London: Fulton. A book for all readers. The education of children who have physical disabilities.

Humphries, S. & Gordon, P. (1992) *Out of Sight*. Plymouth: Northcote. A very powerful book that deals with the experience of being disabled between 1900 and 1950. Plenty of photographs and interviews. If you only look at one book about children with SEN, this should be it. The progress made since the first half of the century is substantial. This is a Channel 4 book that accompanied the TV series *Out of Sight*.

Goldstein, D. (1989) *The Hearing Impaired Child*. Windsor: NFER-Nelson. A useful basic text covering causes, effects, aids and educational implications.

Shah, R. (1992) (Revised 1995) *The Silent Minority*. London: National Children's Bureau. About Asian children who have disabilities. Helps to increase understanding of the special needs of Asian children and their families.

Tucker, I. & Powell, C. (1991) *The Hearing Impaired Child and School*. London: Souvenir. Useful general introduction. Written for parents in particular.

Wolfendale, S. (ed.) (1997) *Meeting Special Needs in the Early Years*. London: Fulton. Various authors discuss policy and practice. For all those who work with very young children.

Chapter 3

Closs, A. (ed.) (2000) *The Education of Children with Medical Conditions*. London: Fulton.

Cogher, L. *et al.* (1992) *Cerebral Palsy*. London: Chapman and Hall. Very thorough text covering development, assessment and therapy.

Donaldson, M. (1995) *Children with Language Impairments*. London: Kingsley. A very good introduction to the subject. Clearly written.

Doyle, J. (1996) *Dyslexia: An introductory guide*. London: Whurr. As the title says, an introduction. Description of dyslexia, identification and assessment of children who have dyslexia. Very useful.

Frith, U. (1989) *Autism*. Oxford: Blackwell. A thorough examination of autism.

Jordan, R. & Jones, G. (1999) *Meeting the Needs of Children with Autistic Spectrum Disorders*. London: Fulton. Compact book that should be of particular help to people working with children with autism for the first time.

Oliver, M. (1996) *Understanding Disability*. London: MacMillan.

Riddick, B. (1996) *Living with Dyslexia*. London: Routledge. What life is like living with children who have dyslexia. How to support them.

Webster, A. & Wood, D. (1989) *Children with Hearing Difficulties*. London: Cassell. The impact of deafness on all aspects of a child's life.

White, A. (2001) *Special Needs*. London: Heinemann.

Chapter 4

Babbage, R. *et al.* (1999) *Approaches to Teaching and Learning*. London: Fulton. Including pupils with learning difficulties.

Best, A. (1992) *Teaching Children with Visual Impairments*. Milton Keynes:

Open University. Practical guide to helping children with visual impairment to gain access to the curriculum.

Chazan, M. *et al.* (1991) *Helping Five-to-Eight Year Olds with SEN.* Oxford: Blackwell.

Dawkins, J. (1991) *Models of Mainstreaming for Visually Impaired Pupils.* London: RNIB/HMSO. Plenty of detailed case studies of integration.

Fraser, B. (1996) *Supporting Children with Hearing Impairment in Mainstream Schools.* London: Franklin Watts. A slim volume providing a clear, straightforward account of causes, identification, aids and support in mainstream school.

Gascoigne, E. (1995) *Working with Parents as Partners in SEN.* London: Fulton.

Kersner, M. & Wright, J. (1993) *How to Manage Communication Problems in Young Children.* London: Fulton. Overview of speech and language development. How to recognise problems.

Hanko, G. (1985) (Second ed. 1990) *Special Needs in Ordinary Classrooms.* Oxford: Blackwell.

Hansmann, H. (1992) *Education for Special Needs.* Edinburgh: Floris. Camphill schools (for children with SEN). The principles and practices of these schools, which are based on the ideas of Rudolf Steiner. Readable and interesting.

Hornby, G. (2000) *Improving Parental Involvement.* London: Cassell. Practical ideas on ways to improve the involvement of parents in schools.

Jenkinson, J. (1997) *Mainstream or Special?* London: Routledge. UK and USA debate.

Lear, R. (1977) (Third ed. 1993) *Play Helps.* Oxford: Butterworth-Heinemann. A very practical book crammed with ideas for creating toys, introducing activities for children with SEN.

Lennox, D. (1991) *See Me After School.* London: Fulton. A book for teachers and students. How to diagnose and help pupils who have emotional and behavioural difficulties (EBD).

McConkey, R. & McGinley, P. (1990) *Innovations in Leisure and Recreation for People with a Mental Handicap.* Chorley: Lisieux Hall. Covers a wide range of activities and ideas with information about providers.

Rose, R. et al. (eds.) (1994) *Implementing the Whole Curriculum for Pupils with Learning Difficulties.* London: Fulton. Written by teachers. Examples of good practice in curriculum design and delivery for pupils with severe learning difficulties.

Wilson, R. (1998) *Special Educational Needs in the Early Years.* London: Routledge. Some case studies showing different ways of interacting.

Chapter 5

Balshaw, M. (1991) *Help in the Classroom*. London: Fulton. Gives insight into the role of learning support assistants (LSAs) in schools.

Fox, G. (1998) *A Handbook for Learning Support Assistants*. London: Fulton.

Chapter 6

Armstrong, F. *et al.* (2000) *Inclusive Education*. London: Fulton. A look at inclusion in several countries.

Clements, P. & Spinks, T. (1994) *The Equal Opportunities Guide*. London: Kogan Page. Full of information on all aspects of the subject. The section on Disability is particularly relevant.

Garner, P. & Sandow, S. (1995) *Advocacy, Self-Advocacy and Special Needs*. London: Fulton. Wide-ranging discussion of this important issue with some good examples of practice in schools.

George, D. (1995) *Gifted Education*. London: Fulton. Examines the meaning of 'gifted'. Identification and how to address needs.

Judd, D. (1995) *Give Sorrow Words*. Whurr Publications.

Koshy, V. & Casey, R. (1997) *Effective Provision for Able and Exceptionally Able Children*. London: Hodder and Stoughton. A very useful text.

Middleton, L. (1999) *Disabled Children: Challenging Social Exclusion*. Oxford: Blackwell. The experience – and difficulty – of being disabled. Discussion of inclusion.

Rieser, R. & Mason, M. (1990) (Revised 1992) *Disability Equality in the Classroom*. London: ILEA. Republished by Disability Equality Education (1992). Lively study on equality with contributions from young people.

SENTC (1996) *Professional Development to Meet Special Educational Needs*. London: SENTC. The subject is teacher education. A report about what teachers need to know if they are to teach children who have SEN. Well worth reading.

Websites

There are hundreds of relevant websites, as you will know. Here is a small selection to point you in the right direction in your search for further information. Often, you will just have to type a keyword to find a helpful site (e.g. Down's syndrome, autism).

This short list of sites is ordered according to general usefulness.

Department for Education & Skills (DFES)
www.DFES.gov.uk (general)
www.DFES.gov.uk/SEN (special educational needs)

Government Disability site
www.Disability.gov.uk

CAF Directory. Excellent directory of medical conditions and support groups. Updated regularly.
www.cafamily.org.uk

National Association for SEN (NASEN)
www.nasen.og.uk

European Agency for the Development of Special Needs Education
www.european-agency.com

Centre for Studies on Inclusive Education (CSIE)
www.inclusion.uwe.ac.uk

BBC Disability Pages
www.bbc.co.uk/radio4/disability

Inclusive Technology. Software & Hardware.
www.inclusive.co.uk

Appendix 2
Useful Addresses

You may wish to find further information. The following list of addresses may help you. Organisations are listed in alphabetical order. This is not necessarily the most helpful way of listing them, but it is the simplest.

ADD-ADHA Family Support
Group UK
1a High Street
Dilton Marsh
Westbury
Wiltshire BA13 4DL

Advisory Centre for
Education Ltd
1B Aberdeen Studios
22/24 Highbury Grove
London N5 2EA

AFASIC
347 Central Markets
Smithfield
London EC1A 9NH

Association for Dance Movement
Therapy
Hertfordshire College of Art &
Design
7 Hatfield Road
St Albans
Herts AL1 3RS

Association of Educational
Psychologists
3 Sunderland Road
Gilesgate
Durham DH1 2LH

Association for Spina Bifida
& Hydrocephalus (ASBAH)
42 Park Road
Peterborough
Cambs PE1 2UQ

British Association of Art Therapists
11a Richmond Road
Brighton
Sussex BN2 3RL

British Association & College of
Occupational Therapists
6/8 Marshalsea Road
London SE1 1HL

British Diabetic Association
10 Queen Anne Street
London W1M 0BD

British Epilepsy Association
Anstey House
Gateway Drive
Yeadon
Leeds LS19 7XY

British Society of Audiology
c/o Hearing Services
General Hospital
Nottingham NG1 6HA

British Society for Music Therapy
25 Rosslyn Ave
East Barnet
Herts EN4 8DH

Brittle Bone Society
30 Guthrie Street
Dundee DD1 5BS

Cancer & Leukemia in
Childhood (CLIC)
12–13 King's Square
Bristol BS2 8JH

Chartered Society of Physiotherapy
14 Bedord Row
London WC1R 4ED

Coeliac Society
POB 220
High Wycombe
Bucks HP11 2HY

Computer Software for SEN
KCS Ltd
POB 700
Southampton
Hants SO17 1LQ

Conductive Education,
Foundation for
Cannon Hill House
Russell Road
Birmingham B13 8RD

Cornelia De Lange Syndrome
CDLS Foundation UK
'Tall Trees'
106 Lodge Lane
Grays
Essex RM16 2UL

Council for Disabled Children
National Children's Bureau
8 Wakley Street
London EC1V 7QE

CSIE – Centre for Studies on
Integration in Education
1 Redland Close
Elm Lane
Redland
Bristol BS6 6UE

Cystic Fibrosis Trust
11 London Road
Bromley
Kent BR1 3RS

Deafblind UK
10 Bridge Street
Peterborough
PE14 1DY

Department for Education
& Skills (DFES)
Sanctuary Buildings
Great Smith Street
London SW1P 3BT

Department of Education
& Science (DES)
Elizabeth House
York Road
London SE1 7PH

Disability Alliance
Universal House
88–94 Wentworth Street
London E1 7SA

Disabled Living Foundation
380–384 Harrow Road
London W9 2HU

Disability Sports England
13–27 Brunswick Place
London N1 6DX

Down's Syndrome Association
155 Mitcham Road
London SW17 9PG

Dyslexia Association
98 London Road
Reading
Berks RG1 5AU

Dyspraxia Trust
8 West Alley
Hitchin
Herts SG5 1EG

Equal Opportunities Commission
Overseas House
Quay Street
Manchester M3 3HN

Health Service Careers
POB 19B
East Molesey
Surrey KT8 0PE

HMSO Books
Publications Centre
51 Nine Elms Lane
London SW8 5DR

Jubilee Sailing Trust
POB 180
The Docks
Southampton
Hampshire SO9 7NF

Leukaemia Care
14 Kingfisher Court
Vinny Bridge
Pinhoe
Devon EX4 8JN

Makaton Vocabulary Development
Project
31 Firwood Drive
Camberley
Surrey GU15 3QD

MENCAP (Royal National Society
for Mentally Handicapped Children
& Adults)
123 Golden Lane
London EC1Y 0RT

Muscular Dystrophy Group of
GB & NI
7–11 Prescott Place
London SW4 6BS

National Association for Able
Children in Education
Westminster College
Oxford OX2 9AT

National Association for SEN
(NASEN)
4–5 Amber Business Village
Amber Close,
Amington
Tamworth
Staffs B77 4RP

National Asthma Campaign
Providence House
Providence Place
London N1 1NT

National Autistic Society
393 City Road
London EC1V 1NG

National Portage Association
127 Monks Dale
Yeovil
Somerset BA21 3JE

Play Matters (information on play &
special needs)
68 Churchway
London SW1 1LT

Prader-Willi Syndrome Association
2 Wheatsheaf Close
Horsell
Woking
Surrey GU21 4BP

Restricted Growth Association
POB 8
Countesthorpe
Leicester LE8 5ZS

Rett Syndrome Association
113 Friern Barnet Road
London N11 3EV

Riding for the Disabled Association
(RDA)
Avenue R, NAC
Stoneleigh
Kenilworth
Warwickshire CV8 2LY

Royal Association for Disability &
Rehabilitation (RADAR)
12 City Forum
250 City Road
London EC1V 8AF

Royal College of Speech &
Language Therapists
7 Bath Place
Rivington Street
London EC2A 3DR

Royal Institute for the Blind
224 Great Portland Street
London W1N 6AA

Royal National Institute for the
Deaf
19–23 Featherstone Street
London EC1Y 8SL

SCOPE
6 Market Road
London N7 9PW

Sense (Deafblind/Rubella Damaged)
11–13 Clifton Terrace
London N4 3SR

Sherborne Research Centre
The Learning Centre
Devenish Road
Ascot
Berks SL5 9PG

Skill (National Bureau for Students
with Disabilities)
18–20 Crucifix Lane
London SE1 3JW

Tourette Syndrome Association
Old Bank Chambers
London Road
Crowborough
E. Sussex TN6 2TT

Index